UNIVERSITY LIBRARY,
UW-STEVENS POINT

# DOMAIN-REFERENCED TESTING

# DOMAIN-REFERENCED TESTING

WELLS HIVELY, EDITOR

EDUCATIONAL TECHNOLOGY PUBLICATIONS
ENGLEWOOD CLIFFS, NEW JERSEY 07632

Library of Congress Cataloging in Publication Data

Hively, Wells, 1931-
    Domain-referenced testing.

    1.   Educational tests and measurements.
2.   Educational surveys.   I.   Title.
LB3051.H57      371.2'6     74-13378
ISBN 0-87778-075-7

The contents of this book were printed originally in the June, 1974 issue of *Educational Technology* Magazine.

Copyright © 1974 Educational Technology Publications, Englewood Cliffs, New Jersey 07632.

All rights reserved. No part of this book may be reproduced or transmitted, in any form or by any means, electronic or mechanical, including photocopying, recording, or by any information storage and retrieval system, without permission in writing from the Publisher.

Printed in the United States of America.

Library of Congress Catalog Card Number:
74-13378.

International Standard Book Number:
0-87778-075-7.

*First Printing: October, 1974.*

## Table of Contents

**Part One: Basic Ideas** ................................................................ 3
   Introduction to Domain-Referenced Testing—Wells Hively ................................................................................. 5
   Beyond Objectives: Domain-Referenced Tests for Evaluation and Instructional Improvement—Eva L. Baker ..................................................................................... 16
   Sampling Plans for Domain-Referenced Tests—Jason Millman ................................................................................. 31

**Part Two: Applications and Innovations** ........................ 43
   Test-Item Domains and Instructional Accountability—Donald B. Sension and George J. Rabehl ..................... 45
   Content, Items, Decisions: Orienting Curriculum-Assessment Surveys to Curriculum Management and Modification—Donald M. Miller ..................... 63
   Teacher Evaluation and Domain-Referenced Measurement—W. James Popham ............................................. 80
   Planning for Evaluation in Performance Contracting Experiments: The Connection to Domain-Referenced Testing Theory—Guilbert C. Hentschke and Donald M. Levine ............................................................ 85
   Program and Product Evaluation from a Domain-Referenced Viewpoint—Thomas J. Johnson ..................... 97

Using Domain-Referenced Tests for Student Placement, Diagnosis and Attainment in a System of Adaptive, Individualized Instruction—Anthony J. Nitko and Tse-Chi Hsu .................................................................. 108

Tracking Behavioral Growth: Day-to-Day Measures of Frequency Over Domains of Performance—Ann Dell Duncan ................................................................. 123

**Part Three: Perspectives** ............................................................. 135
    Some Comments—Wells Hively .......................................... 137
    Some Helpful Sources—Wells Hively .................................. 149

# DOMAIN-REFERENCED TESTING

# PART ONE

# BASIC IDEAS

# Introduction to Domain-Referenced Testing

## Wells Hively

Most of us know that something is wrong with typical attempts to utilize behavioral objectives in education. Most of the time the results turn out to be trivial and artificial. On the other hand, we know that standardized tests are essentially worthless for evaluating instruction or for helping individuals learn more efficiently.

To help learners we need measures that show day-to-day progress in well-defined areas of knowledge and skill. But until recently we have had no comprehensive models to guide us in the construction and validation of such measures. Confusion reigns among educators. Should we base evaluation programs on behaviorally stated goals or should we stay with standardized tests? It is often difficult to interpret the results in either case. We are constantly confused about the relationship of behavioral goals to test construction and test score interpretation.

We need a better understanding of the ingredients that make up comprehensive behavioral formulations of educational accomplishment. For this purpose we need a clearer theory of measurement and a technology to make it operational. That is what Domain-Referenced Testing is about.

The world of psychometrics may be seen as a contrast between Domain-Referenced Testing and Norm-Referenced Testing. The dis-

Wells Hively directs Spaulding Youth Center, Tilton, New Hampshire.

tinction is essentially the same as the one Robert Glaser made between Norm-Referenced Testing and Criterion-Referenced Testing. But the term "criterion" lends itself to misinterpretation. It carries surplus associations to mastery learning that are best avoided by using the more general term "domain" instead. Most people who talk about Criterion-Referenced Testing assume that the technology of Domain-Referenced Testing exists, but they often do not fully recognize what that would imply (see Part Three of this book).

Let's call Domain-Referenced Testing and Norm-Referenced Testing DRT and NRT for short. To build up some intuitive distinctions between DRT and NRT, imagine a shooting range where you could try your skill on flying targets. If the testing program were set up on a DRT model the attendant might begin by showing you a map of the shooting range and introducing it as follows:

"Welcome to the Sure-Fire Shooting Range. We aim for you to learn a lot here about your strengths and weaknesses in wing shooting. X marks the spot where you will stand. Clay pigeons may be released from any of the points shown on the map, ranging (as you can see) from as close as 10 feet to as far away as 50 feet. Standard clay disks may be thrown in any of the directions shown: toward you, away from you, crossing or quartering. We'll throw them at different speeds from 10 feet-per-second to 40 feet-per-second, and the time between releases of successive targets may vary between one second and 10 seconds. Each test sample will consist of 10 throws, and this loud sound will tell you the moment when each target is released. According to our analysis, this domain includes the main characteristics involved in 80 percent of the situations encountered by hunters shooting birds in the field. When you're ready, call for the first series by saying 'pull.'"

After you shoot the first series, the attendant might report the results as follows:

"You did pretty well. If you keep on shooting about as well as you are shooting now, the chances are you will hit about 60 percent of all targets we can throw. You do best on targets that cross from right to left and worst on targets thrown toward you. As you go on shooting, you will probably warm up and improve your percentage a little. From this small sample, we can't tell much more than that, but if you want a more thorough diagnosis try another series."

A shooting range like this, where the domain of problems is clearly defined, provides you, the learner, with abundant information to use in

*Introduction* 7

systematic self-improvement. You can keep shooting until your strengths and weaknesses are clearly diagnosed in terms of distances, directions, velocities and even tricky target sequences. You can practice on the tough ones and follow your growth as it changes day to day in the proportions of various kinds of targets you can hit. You can measure your over-all skill as the probability that you can hit a randomly chosen sequence of targets. You do not need to worry about how your performance compares to the performance of anyone else.

It is not difficult to imagine similar "shooting ranges" for mathematics, reading, musical performance and a wide variety of other important areas. The technology of Domain-Referenced Testing is devoted to the construction and operation of such "shooting ranges."

Now imagine what you might encounter if the shooting range were set up on a NRT model. The attendant might give you the following instructions:

"Welcome to the Wing Shot Testing Range. Here you can compare your skill with that of the other hunters you are likely to meet in the field. X marks the spot where you should stand. Targets may be released from any place in the general area shown. The test will consist of a sequence of 10 targets, released at varying intervals, typifying problems often encountered by bird hunters. Signal when you are ready by saying 'pull.' "

At the end of the test you might be given the following report:

"You did pretty well. With respect to a norm group of 1,000 hunters whose bird licenses had been valid for at least three consecutive years prior to 1970, you scored at the 70th percentile: 30 percent of the hunters shot a better score than you did. With respect to a population of typical young American males, represented by a sample of Armed Forces inductees tested in 1971, your score was at the 85th percentile."

And that is where it *ends* with NRT. The distinctive thing about Norm-Referenced Tests is that the way the sample problems were generated *is not clearly specified*. Therefore, it is impossible to call up an indefinite number of parallel tests, as in the preceding example, by systematically sampling from among the different types of problems. Only three or four "forms" of the test exist, and these must be carefully kept secret. Therefore you, the learner, have no opportunity to practice and to test yourself from day to day on similar examples. And you have no meaningful way to represent your skill except in comparison to the norm groups. A clearly specified, theoretical domain of competence simply does not exist.

That is the intuitive difference between DRT and NRT. DRT has something NRT does not, and it is something that is tremendously important to the learner. This extra something may not seem important if the major purpose of testing is to assign children to groups for instruction, to select young people for employment, or to predict their future (relative) success in higher education. NRT is excellent for those purposes. But if the purpose is to keep track of day-to-day progress and to study the conditions that facilitate or inhibit it, then NRT, as it is universally practiced in American schools, is useless.

It is not easy to build a comprehensive and valid DRT shooting range for the knowledge that we try to teach children in school, but it is by no means impossible. The companion chapters in Part One of this book provide an introduction to how-to-do-it. The chapters in Part Two give an account of some contemporary try-outs, successes and problems in DRT's practical application. In the rest of this introduction, we will sketch some of the more formal characteristics of DRT and NRT, suggest some of their conceptual roots in the fields of Experimental and Differential Psychology and define some terms used in the other chapters.

Figure 1 contrasts the methods used to develop DRT with those used to develop NRT. Both begin with the same raw material: (1) a more-or-less vaguely described universe of knowledge and (2) a more-or-less roughly defined population of experts and learners. The test construction process begins with interviews of experts and learners, and observations of their performance. From these, the constructor of the test collects prototypical items and lays them out according to a rough theory of the subject matter structure. The structure insures that the collection of items covers the range of important situations encountered in the field. At the beginning, it often simply consists of a list of topical headings, with examples of items at various levels of difficulty under each topic.

At this point DRT and NRT diverge. In DRT the goal is to create an extensive pool of items that represents, in miniature, the basic characteristics of some important part of the original universe of knowledge. One tries to construct the pool in such a way that a student who has learned to respond correctly to its items could generalize easily to the field. The basic notions that guide this activity are those of

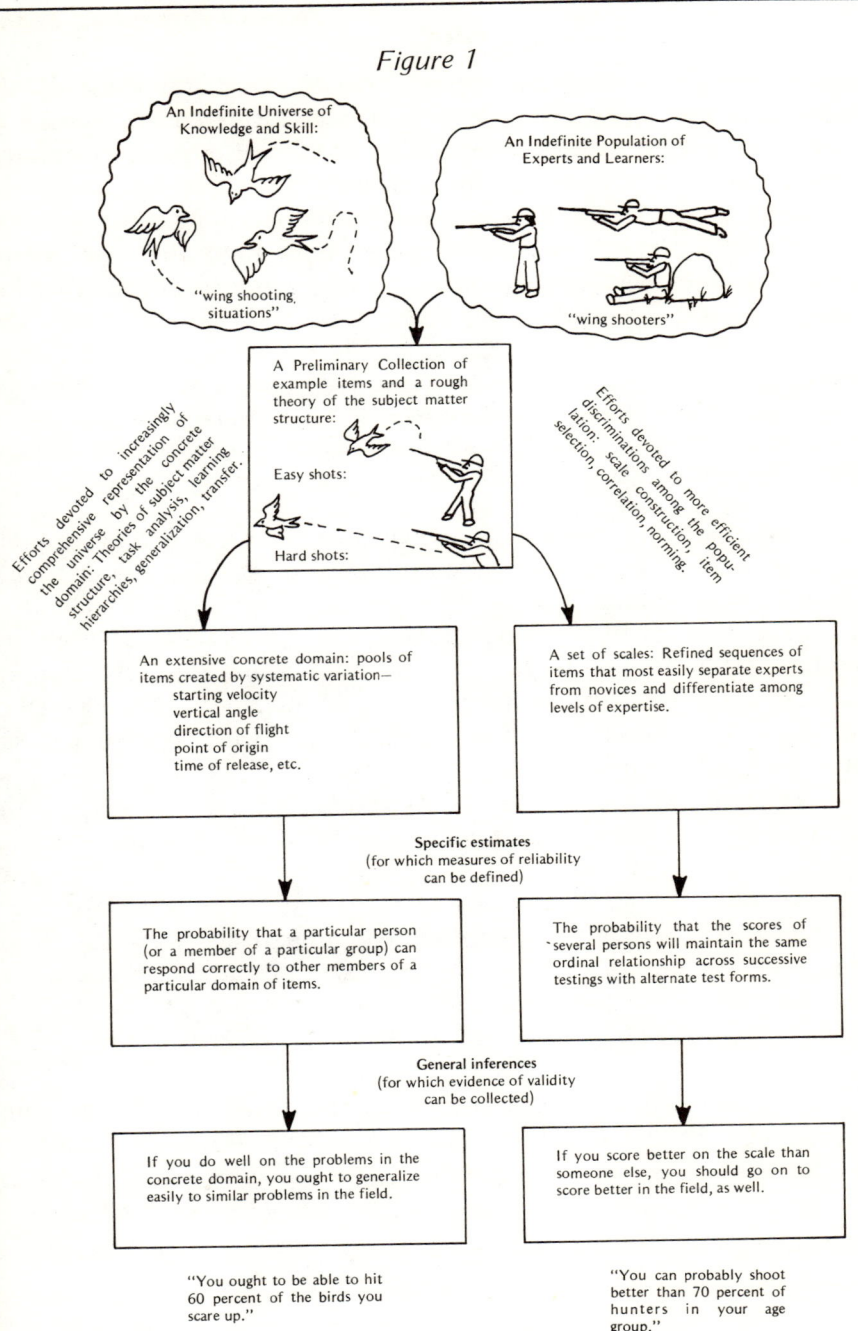

generalization, transfer and subject matter structure. Most of the theoretical and empirical work in Domain-Referenced Testing is devoted to making the concrete domain more and more representative of the essential skills in the original universe.

Because the items in a domain must incorporate the essential characteristics of problems encountered in the field, the term "item" refers to any measurable bit of human performance: spoken, written or athletic, not just paper-and-pencil tasks.

DEFINITION: An "item" is a set of instructions telling how to evoke, detect and score a specific bit of human performance. It must include directions for (1) presenting the stimuli, (2) recording the response and (3) deciding whether or not the response is appropriate.

Sometimes the items in a domain may be generated in a purely empirical way. For example, a shooting range designer could simply follow hunters around, taking observations in the field and include in his domain all of the points of origin and directions of flight he encountered over a considerable period of time. Similarly, a quite practical domain for reading might consist of the front pages from all of last year's local newspapers (Ann Dell Duncan will have more to say about such a domain for reading in Part Two).

An alternative to the empirical collection of typical items is the logical approach—using a systematic combination of speeds, vertical angles, directions of flight, points of origin, times of release, etc., to lay out the range. Similarly, the words on the front pages of last year's newspaper may be grouped according to grammatical categories, phonic rules and frequencies of occurrence. Each of these theoretically important characteristics subdivides the larger domain into smaller ones which may come in handy for purposes of diagnosis and specific practice.

The same item may be a member of several different sub-domains according to the characteristics used to classify it. It may, for example, be a member of the set of "high-velocity throws" and also a member of the set of "throws-from-the-'nine-o'clock'-point-of-origin." Whether or not you hit it affects the estimates of your chances of success on future tosses from one or for both of the sub-domains.

DEFINITION: A "domain" may consist of any clearly specified set of items.

*Introduction*

A useful way to generate domains is to ask what parts of an item can be changed to create other items that test the same general ability. The permissible replacements for the variable elements are then listed, and we can write a set of substitution rules enabling the test maker or even a computer to generate this set of related items.

**DEFINITION**: A list of rules for generating a set of related items is called an "item form."

Figure 2 is a sketch of an item form from an elementary school mathematics program. The "shell" tells the person presenting the item what to say. The blank in the "script" portion of the shell may be filled with any of the replacements shown in the "cell matrix" that follows. To generate an item, look to find the variable (a) in the script. Then, from the corresponding line of the cell matrix, choose one of the three possible phrases to complete the script. Next, from the row beneath choose a numeral (or numerals, $b_1$ and $b_2$) to complete the phrase. In Cell 1, for example, the numeral may range from 0 to 19. A complete script for Cell 1 would be, "tell me a number that is greater than four." An example from Cell 4 would be, "tell me a number that is greater than 4 but less than 5." The shell and the replacement rules together make up the item form. The item form generates a clearly defined set of items within each of the specified cells.*

After a domain has been defined, the actual testing procedure involves drawing samples. The trick is to do this in such a way as to obtain good estimates of the probability that people could respond correctly to all items. Estimates for large domains may be obtained by stratified sampling over their constituent sub-domains, and diagnostic profiles may be gathered by sampling within sub-domains. The problems are the same as those encountered in survey sampling.

Although designing efficient schemes to obtain several different estimates at the same time may be a challenging task, the basic ideas are very simple. (Jason Millman describes them in his chapter.)

In Domain-Referenced Testing, the notion of "reliability" has to do with the accuracy with which one can estimate the probabilities of

---

*W. Hively, G.M. Maxwell, G.J. Rabehl, D.B. Sension and S. Lundin. *Domain-Referenced Curriculum Evaluation*. Los Angeles: Center for the Study of Evaluation, University of California, 1973.

## Figure 2

**ITEM FORM SHELL**

| DIRECTIONS: | SCRIPT: |
|---|---|
| Read script to child: | Tell me a number that is _____ (a) _____ |
| Write down child's exact words. | |

**CELL MATRIX**

| | 1 | 2 | 3 | 4 |
|---|---|---|---|---|
| Script (a) | "greater than $(b_1)$" | "less than $(b_1)$" | "greater than $(b_1)$ but less than $(b_2)$" | |
| Numerals (b) | $0 \leq b_1 \leq 19$ | $1 \leq b_1 \leq 20$ | $0 \leq b_1 \leq 18$ and $(b_1 + 2) \leq b_2 \leq 20$ | $0 \leq b_1 \leq 19$ and $b_2 = b_1 + 1$ |

correct performance within a concrete domain. "Validity" has to do with the success of generalization from performance on a concrete domain to performance in the larger universe of knowledge from which the domain was generated.

Now let us go back and consider the genesis of Norm-Referenced Tests (shown in the right side of Figure 1). Here the main goal is to construct a scale that differentiates among the members of the initial population of experts and learners. Starting with the preliminary collection of example items, the constructor of the test selects and refines them to make up the scale. Items which nearly everybody answers right do not distinguish among the people and so are eliminated; the same thing goes for items which nearly everybody misses. For NRT it is not important to measure what most people *can* do, or what they ideally *ought* to be able to do. It is only necessary to concentrate on what some can do and others cannot. The basic notions

## Introduction

that guide this effort are psychometric scaling, latent-trait analysis and correlational techniques. A scale is a good one, in classic terms, if individuals obtain the same relative scores on its alternative forms (that makes it reliable) and if relative scores on the scale correlate with relative performance in the field (that makes it valid).

Since the focus is on the success of the items in differentiating among people, it is not necessary in NRT to be very specific about the subject matter structure. All that is required is a reasonable correlation between success on each item and success on the test as a whole. It does not matter if items in the scale present a biased picture of the over-all universe, or even if they represent behavior which is not obviously part of the universe at all. They only need to predict relative success effectively. Therefore, items may be selected for their ease of administration rather than for their formal correspondences to the original universe.

In NRT, there need be little emphasis on transfer and generalization. If you learned all answers to items in a Norm-Referenced Test, few people would think that you had learned anything very important. Rather, there would be concern that you had invalidated the scale. In DRT the learner may be told exactly how the items are generated, or he may be given the rules to generate them himself. Only the specific sample drawn in a given testing need be kept secret. By contrast, since there is no generative principle, the items in a Norm-Referenced Test cannot be made public, and the learner may be given only a vague description of the general subject matter that the test "covers." If you want to check whether a testing system is NRT or DRT just ask whether you can have a copy of the test to study. Secrecy is the hallmark of NRT.

Now we can see why Norm-Referenced Tests are so hard to use to evaluate instruction. Consider the problem faced by a teacher who seriously tries to use them for that purpose. If he selects a standardized test and looks at the questions on it, he puts himself in an embarrassing position, because he knows that if he directly teaches the answers to those questions he surely will invalidate the scale. But what else should he teach? In attempting to answer that question, he finds himself sketching out a domain of equivalent items.

If he tries to construct a scale of his own rather than using a standardized test, the teacher faces a similar embarrassment. Should he construct it exclusively of items taken directly from his own instruction? If not, then on what basis could he generate other items? The only way to get out of this difficulty and still avoid DRT is to put teaching and test construction into different hands, and to keep the teacher and the test constructor in ignorance of each other's specific content.

"Preserving the independence of the measure" in this way provides a crude basis for inferring that students who do well on a test have some generalizable abilities and not just specific item-responses. However, the workability of this solution must rest upon an *implicit* agreement between the teacher and the test constructor as to the content of the intuitive domain from which the teacher "draws" teaching material and the test constructor "draws" test material. This implicit agreement, which has often caused trouble for students, is (as several of the chapters in Part Two illustrate) now causing trouble for teachers under the pressure of such things as performance-based evaluation and performance contracting.

Broadly speaking, NRT, which has its roots in Individual Differences, collects data that are useful in prediction and selection; while DRT, which has its roots in Learning Theory, collects data that are useful for evaluating growth. Clearly, schools do both. But we should not confound the activities. While acting as educators we should utilize testing procedures which measure our effectiveness as directly as possible. While acting as learners we should utilize procedures which directly measure our progress. When predicting each other's future competitive success we may use any correlates that come in handy, but when we do so we must continually remind ourselves that we are acting as counselors and gate keepers, not as educators or learners. The failure to keep that distinction in mind underlies much confusion in the field of educational evaluation. Predominant use of Norm-Referenced Testing has perpetuated the confusion. We hope that a wider understanding of the basic ideas behind Domain-Referenced Testing will restore the balance.

**The Book Contents**

This book is divided into three sections: Part One, Basic Ideas; Part Two, Applications and Innovations; and Part Three, Perspectives.

Part One begins with the present chapter. Next, in a how-to-do-it chapter, Eva L. Baker explicates the technical contrast between DRT

## Introduction

construction and the commonly accepted rules of thumb used to develop objectives-based tests.

Taking a long jump to the time when a domain of test items has been assembled for a given subject matter area, Jason Millman describes the basic mathematical models for estimating the probabilities of correct performance in the domain, by individuals or groups.

Is DRT too technically complex to be used in the public schools? George J. Rabehl and Donald B. Sension, in the first chapter in Part Two, describe its application in two public school programs and its relationship to continuous achievement monitoring. Their work as members of the public school staff illustrates many problems and potentialities.

Donald M. Miller analyzes the activities involved in assessment of educational systems at the regional level—activities in which the technology of DRT plays a large part.

W. James Popham, in an essay closely related to the papers by Baker and by Rabehl and Sension, emphasizes the importance of DRT in the context of performanced-based teacher evaluation.

Performance contracting has a way of highlighting all the tough issues in educational evaluation. Guilbert C. Hentschke and Donald M. Levine, experienced commentators on the performance-contracting scene, analyze the role that DRT may play in those issues.

Clearly describing and evaluating the effects of educational products is as difficult as writing performance contracts. Thomas J. Johnson discusses how DRT fits into the evaluator's larger framework.

How do you help an individual student wend his way through a complex hierarchy of predefined skills? Anthony J. Nitko and Tse-Chi Hsu, experts in Individually Prescribed Instruction, describe the role of DRT for that purpose.

Everyone knows that B.F. Skinner laid the groundwork of reinforcement theory, teaching machines and behavior modification in the classroom. It may not be so well known that he is also one of the architects of DRT. Ann Dell Duncan's chapter helps to clarify the nature of the bridge between these fields.

Part Three consists of a summary chapter by the Editor, followed by a listing of relevant source material.

# Beyond Objectives:
# Domain-Referenced Tests
# for Evaluation and
# Instructional Improvement

Eva L. Baker

The noise which has surrounded the advocacy and abuse of behavioral objectives in education persists. Over a decade after Mager (1962) produced his popular how-to-do-it book, the topic is still a focus for symposia, conferences and, in some states, legislative mandates. Contestants for the hearts of educators, in their vigorous arguments for or against the use of behavioral objectives, have apparently lost sight of the limited potential for good or evil that this activity has. So perhaps a brief reprise is in order.

Supporters claim three major functions of behavioral objectives: (1) to aid in the design of more efficient instructional programs; (2) to provide a basis for evaluating the effects of programs; (3) to help clarify the purposes of education and identify unimportant or illusory instructional goals. My bias has always been toward the first purpose: objectives should help one decide about the suitability of different instructional programs and find ways to improve them. However, it is the second purpose which has assaulted the imagination of the public accountability crowd. If goals, criteria and measures can be specified, a reasonable basis for evaluating the effects of the schools may be at hand, so the argument goes. When objectives-based evaluation is used in a summative sense (Scriven, 1967) few questions may be raised—as long

Eva L. Baker is at the University of California, Los Angeles.

*Beyond Objectives*

as an effort is also made to assure that unanticipated outcomes, such as student attitude and teacher satisfaction, are assessed along with the originally planned objectives. Summative evaluation may not pose serious problems because few specific instructional modifications are implied as a consequence of the data analyses.

## Inadequacy of Behavioral Objectives

But the data collected for accountability can have a formative as well as summative intent; as a consequence of evaluations, teachers are expected to improve what they are doing, somehow to get better results. However, the use of objectives as a basis for instructional redesign may not be straightforward and may have, in fact, some negative consequences.

Objectives consist of two main elements: substance and form. The substance of an objective relates to the content to which the learner is to respond. It corresponds generally to the *stimuli* in psychological concepts of learning.

Traditionally, content has served as a major focus for planning school programs. Curricula were organized according to concepts and topics, and the manner in which the student was to demonstrate acquisition of the content was not seen to be critical. In the last decade, the objectives movement has shifted the emphasis to *form*. How the learner displays what he learned—the behaviors that he or she could demonstrate—has become more important. Over-emphasizing either substance or form may inhibit the improvement of instructional practice. Where substance is stressed, it is easy to assume that the manner in which the learner shows his or her understanding is not important. Thus, any manner will do, and testing decays into the selection of the least time-consuming and often least thoughtful manner through which the learner can demonstrate competence.

On the other hand, over-emphasizing the formal, behavioral aspects of objectives may generate a false impression of precision. Because objectives are stated in operational language, they appear to be more teachable. An objective such as "Given a lyric poem, the student will be able to write a 450-word essay on the theme and tone," may look achievable because it follows the much exalted formula: "Given . . . the student will be able to . . . ," but such is not the case.

Because it is easy to transform goals into the accepted format, objectives like the lyric poem example may be casually produced. As long as a "behavioral" verb has been supplied, many consultants and supervisors have little to criticize. Even the more sophisticated may seek only to assign the objective to a higher level category on the *Taxonomy of Educational Objectives* (Bloom et al., 1956). The key problem is this: *most behavioral objectives do not present sufficient cues regarding what a teacher should alter in instruction to facilitate improved learning.*

Test items written to measure behavioral objectives are usually prepared by taking the objective and then trying to produce items that are congruent with its specifications. Given an objective, the test writer tries to produce items which at least incorporate the response condition specified, so that an objective which calls for the student to *select* a response is likely to have with it items where the learner is actually making a choice. But writers typically have difficulty with the stimulus end of the items. Except for broadly defined content, e.g., lyric poems or differential equations, they have few rules to go by. Selection of content is haphazard. Consequently, when teachers are faced with students who do not achieve the objective, they often have grave difficulty in selecting content for practice examples.

Teachers could guess, after inspecting the test, what is the relevant class of examples corresponding to the objective. But the chances of their attending to an irrelevant aspect, i.e., one not in the minds of the objective writer, are high. Teachers might, in desperation, permit students to practice on the actual test items in hopes that the subsequent measure would consist of similar items. Whatever choice the teacher makes, the promise of effective remediation is relatively low.

If typical behavioral objectives do not provide bases for instructional design and remediation, what options are available to an evaluator who is charged with the responsibility of providing data to facilitate instructional improvement? Domain-referenced testing can supply both the data needed for assessment of instructional programs and information suitable for feedback to teachers to facilitate planning.

## Domains and Transferable Skills

A domain consists of a subset of knowledge, skills, understandings or attitudes where the essential attributes of the content which the student is expected to acquire and the behavior through which he or she is expected to demonstrate such acquisition are carefully described. Rather than measuring a single point within the vast universe of knowledge, e.g., "To list four causes of the formation of the Confederate States of America," or a general, but unmanageably broad area, e.g., "To write an essay on civil strife," domains for teaching and testing represent an attempt to find a reasonable compromise between vagueness and over-precision. Domains should function so that a large number of test items could be generated according to given rules and randomly sampled to constitute comparable tests.

The problem of specifying domains for testing can be compared to a more familiar problem in the field of educational psychology: the definition and promotion of transfer skills. Educational goals or objectives seldom should be articulated for the mastery of single items. For instance, an objective where the learner is required to write the analysis of Antony's speech in Shakespeare's *Julius Caesar* cannot in itself be justified. One expects that, if the learner is able to write such an analysis, the ability will transfer to other instances of literature, encountered both within and outside of formal schooling. The danger in specifying an objective similar to the one presented above is that it may be taught in a manner which is likely to result in minimum generalization. Teachers may focus on Antony's speech *qua* Antony's speech; they may frequently ignore, in this situation, pointing up the salient aspects included in his oratory and demonstrating their application in other persuasive writing. The main idea behind transfer of training, the provision of multiple examples, is missing from objectives that focus on a single instance of content. Antony's speech, *David Copperfield*, *Silas Marner*, among numerous other literary classics, were made forgettable for most of us by low-generality teaching of this type.

Domains require the objective-maker to focus on the range of eligible content to which the learner's skill is to apply. Rather than formulate the above objective in terms of Antony's rhetoric, one would instead describe the class of rhetoric his speech represented and attempt to generate rules by which other speeches could be judged as similarly appropriate representatives of the class of rhetoric.

Thus, central to the problem of specifying domains is the definition of content rules or limits. Such rules specify the common characteristics of eligible examples, problems, or more generally, *stimuli* which will be presented to the learner in the testing and teaching situations. The designation of content rules represents the most significant departure of domain-referenced testing from the more common objectives-based evaluation. Thus, the use of domains in the design of instruction and in the design of tests, in effect, prohibits the production of trivial objectives. The force of domain preparation is to influence the writer in the direction of significant, generalizable skills. The ability to list three causes for the depression could only be a suitable objective if, in domain context, it were modified to concern the generalizable causes of economic decline, of which the 1929 depression was only one example.

Content limits may be simple or complex. Examples of simple limits may be derived from the field of mathematics, where it is relatively easy to specify what the replacement set for content is, e.g., "two digit numbers," "fractions where the numerator is one and the denominator less than 100." On the other hand, domains specified for disciplines such as history, e.g., "to analyze in writing a totalitarian government," require a complex set of rules for selection of content, e.g., examples of totalitarian governments might include those drawn from any geographical area, where absolute power was aggregated to a small number of individuals, where individual rights, as exemplified in the U.S. Constitution and amendments, were abrogated without recourse, etc.

The force of such content limits, *under theoretical circumstances*, is not only to provide clear guidance for what is a suitable stimulus for presentation during teaching or testing; one would also expect that performance on content sampled from the domain would be homogeneous. Students should not have any more difficulty in dealing with totalitarianism in 17th century France, 10th century China or 20th century Spain. Even if homogeneity of student response could not be demonstrated, the results of domain specification at minimum is to emphasize the generalizable attributes of the subject matter and to increase the probability of transfer.

## Guidelines for Preparing Domains

If domain-referenced tests are theoretically important, how can those charged with evaluation responsibility learn to prepare such instruments? A simplified version of the production of domain-referenced tests will be presented below. The procedure emphasizes certain aspects of the domains assumed to require most attention. Let us take as a point of departure the rules or guidelines usually prescribed for the production of criterion-referenced tests. Criterion-referenced, or ob-

*Beyond Objectives*

jectives-based, tests ordinarily focus on the following attributes of instructional design:

---

### OBJECTIVES-BASED TESTS

1. Objectives are operationally (behaviorally) stated.

2. Criteria for scoring are provided.

3. Conditions for the administration of the test are described.

4. A sample test item may be given.

---

These guidelines were assembled from books such as Mager's (1962) and materials designed to assist schools with evaluation such as the *Collections* of objectives and measures distributed by the Instructional Objectives Exchange at UCLA.

**Clarifying Substance**

Domain specifications include attributes very similar to those listed for objectives-referenced test design. However, domain specifications require attention to dimensions beyond those normally considered by criterion-referenced design.

---

### ELEMENTS OF DOMAIN SPECIFICATIONS

1. Domain Description
2. Content Limits
3a. Criteria, or
3b. Distractor Domains
4. Format
5. Directions
6. Sample Item

---

Let us proceed sequentially. Domain Descriptions obviously correspond to what are usually termed behavioral objectives.

Domain Description: A general, but operational statement of the behavior and content upon which the test focuses.

The *domain description* term is preferred because the word *objectives* implies *intent*. Tests may also be written to measure in a systematic way performance other than that encompassed in the goals of an instructional program. For instance, an instructional program on transformational grammar could also be evaluated by sampling a domain involving principles of structural grammar as well, to determine the extent of overlap. In most situations, however, the terms "objective" and "domain description" may be interchanged.

The statement of the domain description or objective serves to delimit the general area of concern for the producer of the domain specifications. If the objective calls for the student to "write essays on post-impressionist artists," we know that the area of interest is art rather than mathematics, post-impressionists rather than expressionists and that an essay will be the form in which the response is to be generated. Thus, from the infinite range of content and behavior available to people, the use of an objective or domain description has significantly focused our attention.

The critical and unique aspects of the domain specifications are contained in the next two sections. The first, *Content Limits*, provides a set of rules to describe what content is appropriate to include or to sample in the test or instructional examples. The Content Limits describe the range of content to which the learner is expected to respond.

Content Limits: A set of rules (or a list) of content eligible for inclusion in the test items or in instruction.

There is no component in the objectives-referenced test guidelines which corresponds to the notion of content limits. In effect, the test designer is fencing off the area of content which is considered to be essential in the mastery of the more general domain description or

*Beyond Objectives*

objective. For instance, if the domain description called for the student to diagram standard English sentences, then the content limits for such an objective might contain the following:

---

### CONTENT LIMITS

I.  Sentences in the structural patterns:

| | | |
|---|---|---|
| Noun$_1$-verb-noun$_2$ | Example: | I like you. |
| Noun$_1$-linking verb-noun$_1$ | Example: | Mary is a doctor. |
| Noun-linking verb-adjective | Example: | John has been unhappy. |
| Noun-verb | Example: | The crowd roared. |

II.  Any tense or number may be used.

III.  Patterns may be modified by single or series of adjectives or adverbs.

---

These content limits delineate more precisely sentences which are eligible contenders for correct answers. The teacher or designer, when made aware of such limits, has the following information available:

1. Students are expected to generalize their skills to four basic declarative sentence patterns. They are not expected to be competent with less familiar structures. ($N_1$-V-$N_2$-A: The girls thought him rude.)
2. They should be able to discern appropriate sentence structures regardless of the tense of the sentence of whether the number is singular or plural.
3. They will not be given complex sentences as stimuli. A modified sentence such as this example would be acceptable:

> Quickly and efficiently, the agile freshman forward rebounded the ball.

The next sentence would not:

> With grace and cunning, the runner sidestepped his

opponent, and in a split second, carried the ball over the goal line.

Precision about the class of sentences which should be emphasized can enormously assist the planner of instructional sequences, for the relevant content areas are limited. Instructional time need not be spent parsing complex sentences. It should be devoted to providing a range of relevant models for the learner to confront. Thus, in an instructional improvement situation, where a set of learners has not performed to specified standards, the teacher is much advantaged by having a copy of the rules by which content was selected for inclusion on the instrument. Access to rules is a far different and infinitely more appropriate condition than providing teachers with copies of the test to be used. If Content Limits are defined and disseminated, the teacher has a clear idea of the type of sentence which should appear on the examination, but not the exact set of sentences which *will* appear. Thus, the teacher must teach toward the skill at the transfer or generalization level rather than a rote skill to be drummed methodically into the minds of the students.

The set of content limits in the example provided still allows a wide range. Certain aspects of sentence formation were left to vary freely, such as complexity of vocabulary and familiarity of topic. If desirable for a given instructional program, these aspects could be specified as well. The amount of information the instructional planner has available as a consequence of reasonable content limits is significantly improved from that which is included in the usual instructional objective.

A third critical component of a domain specifications approach to the generation of teaching and testing domains is the statement of criteria for constructed responses.

---

**Criteria for Constructed Responses**: Rules by which the adequacy of response to the item can be judged.

---

A criterion statement has been ordinarily considered as the part of the objective which clarifies what serves as an adequate response. For instance, in an objective where an essay on economic systems is desired, a statement of criteria might describe what points the learner should make in order to be considered correct. For example, the learner might

*Beyond Objectives*

be asked to include political, social and educational consequences of a set of described economic systems. In addition to substantive points, the learner might also be required to provide his or her answers in a particular format, providing references for any statement in standard bibliographic style. Criteria for constructed response, in this way, further specify what is to be taught. For instance, if an important criterion for the above objective relates to the relationship of economic systems to other institutions, then the teacher should include in the instructional program some place for the learner to gain access to needed principles. If bibliographic style were a serious criterion, then instruction relevant to citations, footnotes, etc., would be requisite. The actual implementation of criteria, however, often involves applying standards in evaluating a learner's product beyond what has been taught during the instructional program. Teachers have been known to use talent dimensions such as originality as a basis for evaluating student responses. If such a criterion is included in a statement of a domain, some attempt to operationalize it must be made. The thrust of the domain specifications is to describe clearly what relevant attributes a response should encompass. Where these cannot be well explained, then one might argue that such a dimension is inappropriate for inclusion in teacher evaluation designs, for the chance a teacher has to improve performance is low.

Another problem is posed when the learner is expected to select the correct response from among alternatives. A critical error in the design of tests is often made when the distractors, the presented but incorrect choices, are generated on an unplanned basis. Wrong answers can be described in more detail than "they are not the right ones." In many cases, critical discriminations are important to learning. One does not wish the learner to choose correct answers when presented with *any* set of distractors. One may wish to discern that the learner can choose correctly when presented with the most confusable alternative set. For instance, that a child can choose a "d" from a random selection of other letters may be adequate; however, to test his or her skill at a more sensitive level, one might wish to limit the distractors to those composed of lines and curves (p, r, b) rather than certain readily identifiable letters like x, s, and i.

For selected responses:

Distractor domain: specifies the rules for inclusion of wrong-answer alternatives.

Imagine that you are a teacher whose students have been given an achievement test in the area of chemistry. Suppose you wish to re-teach or remediate students' performances that fall below a certain criterion level. If you understood the multiple-choice test to be developed according to traditional procedures, you could not plan specifically to provide the students with relevant selection practice, for wrong answers might be drawn from the entire range of beginning chemistry. If, on the other hand, you were presented with the rules by which wrong answers were selected, such as equations were imbalanced, -ites and -ates were interchanged, etc., you should be able to see that you would be in a decidedly stronger position. You could not only teach students what the right answers would be but you could also teach them about errors they might be likely to make.

To prepare a section in the domain specifications on distractor domains, the same procedure as for content limits is involved. The rules are specified to delimit the range of wrong answers. The test designer need only to generate an appropriate population of wrong answers and to sample from among them.

## Clarifying Form

In each of the preceding topics, the primary concern was the further clarification of the substantive portion of the objective. One was encouraged to describe rules for the generation of appropriate content; to identify suitable scoring criteria when the task is a constructed one; to define the limits of distractor domains when the response format requires the learner to select responses.

So far, our domain specifications looks like this:

**PARTIAL DOMAIN SPECIFICATIONS**

1. Domain description (objective):

*Beyond Objectives*

2. Content limits:

3a. Criteria (for constructed responses): or

3b. Distractor domains (for selected responses):

---

Two additional components to the domain specifications are required to clarify fully the design for the set of items. These concerns are more similar to typical concerns in test design, and thus will be only briefly treated.

A further clarification of the format of the item, beyond that stated in the Response Description, may be required. If the objective calls for the learner to select from alternatives the correct sum of an addition problem, the form in which the item is presented to the student can seriously influence his or her achievement on it. For instance, if an addition problem is displayed horizontally, 34 + 45 = . . . , the learner may not do as well if his or her previous experience consisted of problems arrayed vertically:  34
 +45

One might argue that the ability to solve addition problems should not be contingent upon their spatial orientation, and I would agree. However, the testing situation is not the time to spring previously unencountered displays on a child. If a range of positions were to be included on the test, these should be specified in the format section of the domain specifications, precisely so that teachers could provide suitable practice situations for their students.

---

**Format:** A description of the form in which the items will be presented to students.

---

A common type of objective calls for the learner to identify an example of concept when presented with a series of distractors, for instance,
   Which of the following is a correct octal number?

      a. 16
      b. 18
      c. 94

The problem becomes more complex, of course, as the number of alternatives increases, for chance correct answering is reduced, reading time expanded, and the individual comparisons the learner must make are increased. The instructional planner should be told whether items are to consist of three, four or five alternatives. She can gear instruction to provide practice in exactly the format or formats to be tested. Thus, the format statement provides a physical description of the item: how long it will be, how many distractors, what additional cues (such as graphs or displays) the learner may have available and (if significant, as in addition) how the items will be arrayed on the page. The purpose of format statements, beyond providing guidance in instruction, is to constrain item writers to adhere to a specified set of rules in order to avoid the introduction of error into the test by varying the properties of the item inadvertently. A second feature of the specifications which serves to control a formal rather than substantive concern is the description of test directions:

---

Directions: Facsimile of directions provided the learner in the test situation.

---

Unfortunately, the provision of carefully planned directions is often overlooked in locally prepared tests. The wording of the directions must be in language that the student can comprehend. The directions should be checked to determine that they do not require the learner to make responses different from those anticipated in the response description.

### Synthesis

The last element of the domain specifications is the inclusion of an item sampled from within the content limits and intended as a representative of the class of response desired. The item should adhere to all rules (content limits, distractor domains, format statement) included in the domain specifications. It merely serves to clarify, by example, what was meant in the various sections. The sample item is not sufficient in itself to serve the clarifying function, for unless augmented by the verbal description of each of the item form elements, the evaluator is forced to again infer, with attending errors, the relevant attributes the item exemplifies.

*Beyond Objectives*

A total plan for domain test specifications is as follows:

---

**WORK SHEET FOR DOMAIN SPECIFICATIONS**

Domain description:
(objective)

Content limits:

      Criteria for constructed responses

          or

      Distractor domains for selected responses

---

Format statement

Directions

Sample item

---

    Most decisions regarding content limits, criteria or distractor domains, formats, etc., are arbitrary, as are most curriculum decisions. The use of domain-referenced tests will have power when decisions regarding goals and content are made according to justifiable rather than incidental bases.

    It is suggested that you take an important objective in your own field, and attempt to prepare domain specifications for it. Only when you begin to interact with the problem can you appreciate some of its difficulty. For this reason, domain specifications are not suggested for across-the-board preparation. Only goals of significance are worthy of the design effort. As a corollary, only goals worthy of adequate test design should actually be measured. The use of domain specifications should be highly selective. If the procedure operates as I think it should, it will reduce the number of specific goals which are formally evaluated and focus on a relatively few but important outcomes. Thus, the drive for evaluating every classroom activity—every instructional encounter—would be reduced and evaluation efforts would assume their proper functions: contributors to the design of effective, significant instruction.

## References

Bloom, B.S., M.D. Engelhart, E.J. Furst, W.H. Hill and D.R. Krathwohl. *Taxonomy of Educational Objectives, Handbook I: Cognitive Domain.* New York: David McKay Co., 1956.

Mager, R.F. *Preparing Instructional Objectives.* Palo Alto, California: Fearon Publishers, 1962.

Scriven, M. The Methodology of Evaluation. *Perspectives of Curriculum Evaluation.* AERA Monograph Series on Curriculum Evaluation, No. 1. Chicago: Rand McNally, 1967.

# Sampling Plans for Domain-Referenced Tests

Jason Millman

After domains of items are defined and groups of examinees identified, we need to set up an efficient assignment plan for the domain-referenced testing program to govern how the examinees encounter the items. Figure 1 provides perspective on the problem: each cell represents a place where a particular examinee may encounter a particular item upon a particular occasion.

An *item* (as noted by Hively, this book) may be any well-defined particle of human performance (answering a multiple-choice question, assembling a tool or playing a passage on a musical instrument), so long as it meets one important requirement: it must be unambiguously scoreable as either correct (a "hit"), incorrect (a "miss") or not attempted (a "skip"). The number of items in a domain may range from just a few to a very large number. Within a large domain they may be grouped together in various subclasses or arranged in hierarchical patterns in a mixture of crossed or nested relationships.

The *examinees* may be any well-defined group of persons, from a small group such as the students exposed to a given instructional program, to a large one such as all the high school students in a region. The over-all group of examinees may be subdivided into classrooms, school districts, groups based on past achievement, and so on. The

**Jason Millman** is at Cornell University, Ithaca, New York.

*Figure 1*
*Potential Testing Situations*

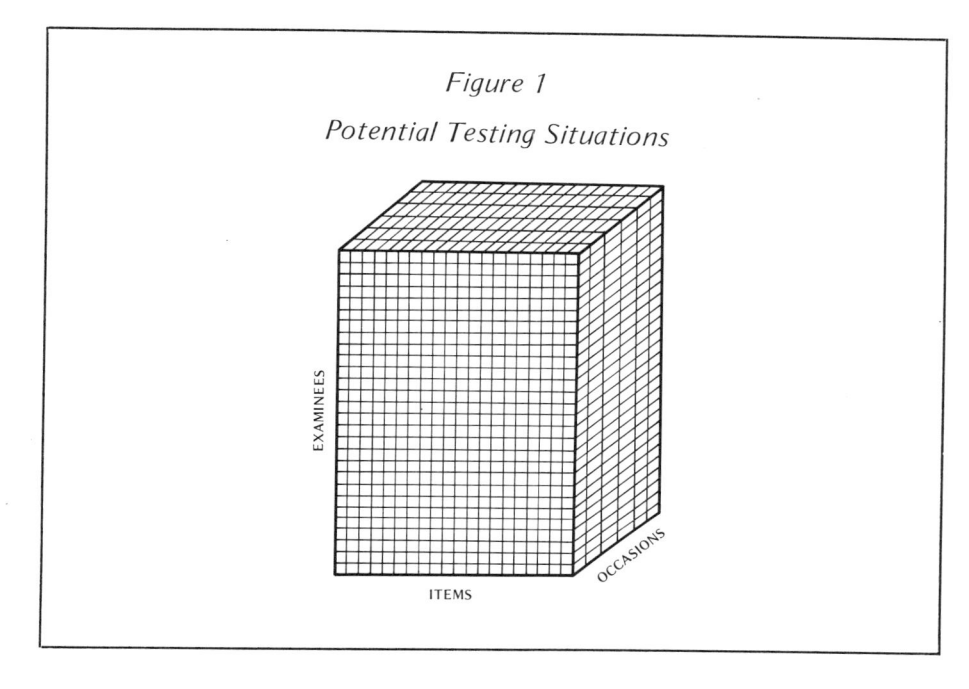

*occasions* are those arranged in a schedule of observation designed to detect the growth or change in which we are interested. In setting up an assignment plan, the problem is to select samples of examinees and arrange for them to encounter samples of items, on a series of occasions, in order to estimate the probability that future encounters of the same kind will be successful.

One might imagine giving all the items in a small domain to everyone in the group; but even if it were possible, it would seldom be worthwhile to administer *every* item to *every* person on *every* occasion. The costs in time and effort to examinees and examiners would ordinarily be prohibitive. Fortunately, the same information can be ascertained, to a high degree of precision, by *sampling* from the cells in Figure 1. How to design such sampling strategies is the focus of this chapter.

What goes into a good assignment plan depends on the purpose of the testing. The two main purposes of testing are usually (1) to make decisions about an examinee or (2) to make decisions about an instructional program.

*Sampling Plans*

**Examinee Evaluation**

One use of domain-referenced achievement tests is to evaluate and make decisions about specific examinees. Such tests might be employed to decide if "certification" should be awarded, to decide if further instruction is required or to keep track of an individual's growth over the domain and project it into the future. When interest is focused on a particular examinee, then the examinee dimension in Figure 1 cannot be sampled. To decide if Joe passes, you must test Joe. However, the items and, for some applications, the occasions can be sampled.

*Comparing an Individual's Score to a Standard.* In many applications a passing score may be established for a domain and a decision (advance or recycle, certify or reject) may be based upon the examinee's performance relative to this standard. For example, suppose the domain of interest consists of the 100 simple addition facts and the passing standard is 85 percent. Although all 100 items could be administered, it would probably be more efficient to compose a test of only a randomly chosen sample—say 40 of the items. The proportion of items passed on the test may be used as an estimate of the proportion of all the items in the domain that the examinee could pass. Thus, if a student answered only 24 of the 40 correct (60 percent), he would not meet the standard.

What are the chances that the above judgment is wrong? To find this out, the range of possible scores may be divided into three regions: pass, uncertain and fail. An example of such regions for the 40-item test with an 85 percent standard is provided in Figure 2.

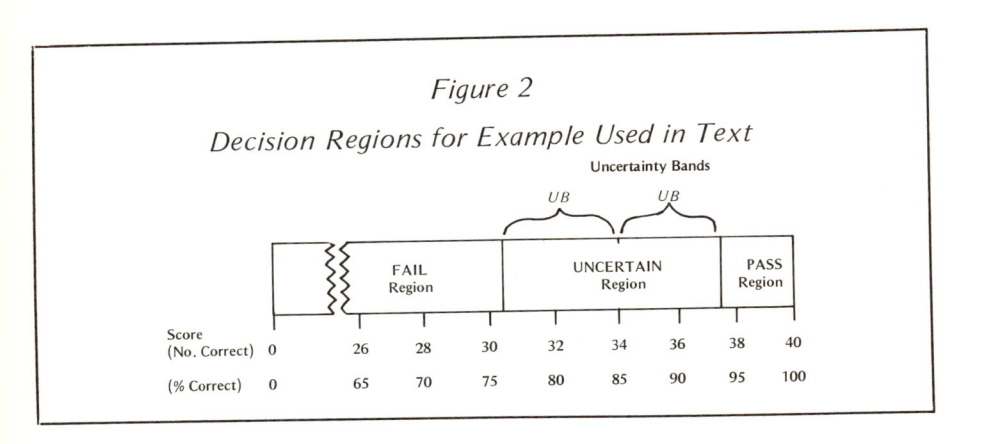

*Figure 2*
*Decision Regions for Example Used in Text*

Uncertainty Bands

| | FAIL Region | UNCERTAIN Region | PASS Region |
|---|---|---|---|
| Score (No. Correct) | 0   26   28   30 | 32   34   36 | 38   40 |
| (% Correct) | 0   65   70   75 | 80   85   90 | 95   100 |

An uncertainty band, *UB*, may be calculated as follows:

$$UB = 2\sqrt{\left[\frac{N-n}{N-1}\right] \frac{P_S (1 - P_S)}{n}}$$

*(Formula 1)*

where
*UB* is the uncertainty band expressed in percent,
*N* is the number of items in the domain,*
*n* is the number of items in test, and
$P_S$ is the passing standard expressed in percent;

When 100, 40 and 85 are substituted respectively for *N*, *n* and $P_S$, UB = 9 percent as indicated in Figure 2. Should an examinee fall into the uncertain zone, more items may be administered, the value of *n* in Formula (1) is then increased accordingly, a smaller uncertainty band computed, and the percent of items the examinee can pass re-estimated using the combined performance of both testings. In this way, we may test sequentially until a confident decision can be made. When scores fall outside of the uncertainty band, correct decisions are made over 95 percent of the time.

When a cell matrix is used to conceptualize a domain of items (see Hively's chapter) it may be possible to make more accurate estimates of a person's domain score. A test more representative of the total domain can be composed when the test items are randomly chosen from each of the subsets defined by the cell matrix. For such stratified item sampling, the estimate of the over-all domain percent score for the examinee is:

$$\hat{P} = \frac{N_1}{N} P_1 + \frac{N_2}{N} P_2 + \ldots + \frac{N_k}{N} P_k = \sum_{i=1}^{k} \frac{N_i}{N} P_i$$

*(Formula 2)*

*If the value of *N* is not known but is considered to be very large, the bracketed term in Formula (1) may be set equal to one.

# Sampling Plans

where
- $\hat{P}$ is the estimated domain score,
- $N_i$ is the number of potential items in the $i$th subset,
- $N$ is the total number of items in the domain and equals $\Sigma N_i$, and
- $P_i$ is the percent of items in the $i$th subset which the examinee has passed.

To illustrate, suppose the domain of 100 items testing the basic arithmetic facts were divided into two sets ($k = 2$), a 25-item subset in which both of the addends may be between 1 and 5 inclusive (i.e., the easier problems) and a 75-item subset composed of items in which one or both of the addends may be zero or 6 through 9 inclusive. (Thus, 4 + 3 would be the first subset, 8 + 7 and 6 + 0 would both be in the second subset.) A 40-item test could be composed of 10 items randomly sampled from the first subset and 30 items from the second, more difficult subset. Now suppose an examinee got all 10 of the first group of items correct but missed five items from the second group. From Formula 2, the examinee's estimated domain score, $\hat{P}$, would be:

$$\hat{P} = \frac{25}{100}(100) + \frac{75}{100}(83.3) = 25 + 62.5 = 87.5,$$

which barely surpasses the 85 percent standard.

If you are working with "domains" defined so that the number of items in each one cannot be clearly stated, the expression ($N_i/N$) in Formula 2 may be replaced by $W_i$, the weight you wish to assign items in the $i$th subset in determining an examinee's domain score. Sometimes even when the exact number of items in each subset is known it makes good sense to assign all the sub-domains equal weight, if they are conceptually of equal importance (independent of the number of items each contains).

The uncertainty band calculated by Formula 1 can be used for the proportion obtained from Formula 2, but this band will often be *slightly* larger (i.e., more conservative) than need be. Formula 5.43 in Cochran (1963) is more precise but the difference will be small unless the average difficulty levels of items in the several strata vary markedly from one another.

*Estimating an Individual's Domain Score, Without Comparing It to a Standard.* Often we may wish to know an individual's domain score without necessarily making an immediate decision about it. Such domain scores might, for example, be provided to students and parents as part of a school's reporting system. As in the preceding section, the examinee's score on a random sample of items may be taken as an estimate of his domain score or, if the test is stratified into subsets, Formula 2 can be used.

In the absence of a fixed standard, the *UB*s will not be precisely symmetrical about an examinee's estimated domain score. For domains in which items are not divided into subsets, the *UB*s can be obtained from tables of a 95 percent confidence interval for a population proportion. Such tables are widely available, see e.g., Marascuilo (1971). For domains whose items are stratified, Formula 2 can be used as an approximation for more accuracy, or, formula 5.43 in Cochran in which the examinee's subtest percent scores, $p_j$, is substituted for the population values.

*Making Comparison Among Two or More Domain Scores for Individual Examinees.* There are three main situations calling for comparisons among domain scores. One, an examinee might be tested on two or more occasions to determine if there has been growth in achievement.* Two, an examinee might be tested with items sampled from two or more domains to map a profile of his abilities. Three, several examinees might be tested with items sampled from the same domain to compare their performance.

In all three applications, each examinee's domain score can be estimated by procedures described above. The *UB* for a difference between two such estimated domain scores is typically larger than the *UB* for any one score. In comparing the scores of two persons on one domain, the *UB* of the difference will be the square root of the sum of the separate squared *UB*s. For example, if the domain scores for two examinees have *UB*s of 3 percent and 4 percent, the *UB* associated with the difference between their two scores is $\sqrt{3\%^2 + 4\%^2} = 5\%$. The *UB*s

---

*One of the greatest utilities of DRT is the ability to generate an indefinite number of samples of items according to the same assignment plan. Scores on each of the tests provide independent estimates of the domain score. If an individual tests himself periodically with a series of such samples he can chart his over-all growth on the domain. Such repeated measurement will be most useful for domains of complex and heterogeneous behaviors where complete mastery is not easily accomplished (see Duncan's chapter).

# Sampling Plans

for the comparisons described in situations (1) and (2) will almost always be smaller, so the calculated value may be used as a conservative approximation. The *UB* decreases as the correlation between the two scores increases.

Should the exact same test be used more than once? Classical test theory tells us that when we compare two people's performance it is advisable to administer the same set of items to both persons. It also advises us, when measuring change for one individual, to balance the risk of practice effect (if the same items are used on the two occasions) against the loss of accuracy resulting from the additional measurement error introduced when different samples of items are used at the two times. The resolution of this balancing "act" depends upon the nature and number of the test items involved—some items are less susceptible to practice than others; expected differences in test difficulty are less when many items are employed in each.

## Program Evaluation

In program evaluation our concern is not so much with how each individual performs for his own sake, but with what his performance implies about the quality of the instruction. The focus is upon domain scores as indicators of relative strengths and weaknesses of the program. Because of this focus, we are freed from the restriction that every student be tested. The examinees as well as the items may be sampled (see Figure 1).

*Item Scores.* In the early stages of program development, data on specific items can be of great help. A random sample of examinees can be administered the items of particular interest or, if more convenient, different samples of examinees can be administered different samples of items. The proportion of people in the sample who pass the item can be taken as the estimate of the difficulty level for the population of examinees. *UB*s for these proportions can be found in charts of the 95 percent confidence intervals for proportions. (We estimate the proportion of people who can answer an item in exactly the same way as we estimate the proportion of items an individual can answer.)

When the population of students is subdivided into classrooms, schools, socioeconomic groups, etc., you may wish to estimate the difficulty of an item by stratified sampling from each of the subgroups. The rationale and method of calculating the population score and the uncertainty band is exactly the same as that previously described for sampling sub-domains to estimate an individual's domain score. That is, the mathematics and formulas are the same whether the problem is to estimate the proportion of items in a domain that can be answered correctly by one student or, as in the present case, the proportion of students in the population that can answer correctly one item.

It is sometimes more convenient, but usually less precise, to administer tests to samples of students in some, but not all, classrooms. Specifically, a random sample of classrooms is chosen and a constant percent of students is randomly selected from each of the classrooms to receive a given item. The estimated difficulty level of the item is given by the proportion of the students answering the item correctly. The $UB$ associated with this sampling plan may be found by taking two times the square root of the formula near the bottom of p. 278 in Cochran (1963).

Several assignment plans were discussed in connection with estimating an item score. As long as students and/or classrooms are selected randomly, the greater the number of students who are administered an item, the more precise the estimate of the proportion of the students in the total population who can answer the item correctly. Especially if test performance is expected to vary from class to class, better estimates will result if a few students are sampled from many classrooms than if many students are chosen from just a few classrooms.

*Estimating Average Domain Scores Across Both Students and Items.* When performance of specific examinees is to be evaluated, our assignment plans involve the sampling of items. When performance on a specific item is of interest, the plans involve sampling of people. In this section, focus is on averages of scores for students in a program and, thus, both items and examinees can be sampled. The discussion is intended to highlight the main possibilities, referring the reader elsewhere for detailed procedures and formulas. Examples of several item-examinee assignment plans (also referred to as matrix sampling plans) are shown in Figure 3.

Diagram (a) in Figure 3 represents a random sample of examinees, each receiving the same test composed of three test items. The mean domain score is estimated by the percent of correct examinee-item responses or, in the case illustrated, by the percentage of the 12 items which are correctly answered. Formula (11.11.6) in Lord and Novick (1968) provides the sampling variance for such domain scores. Two

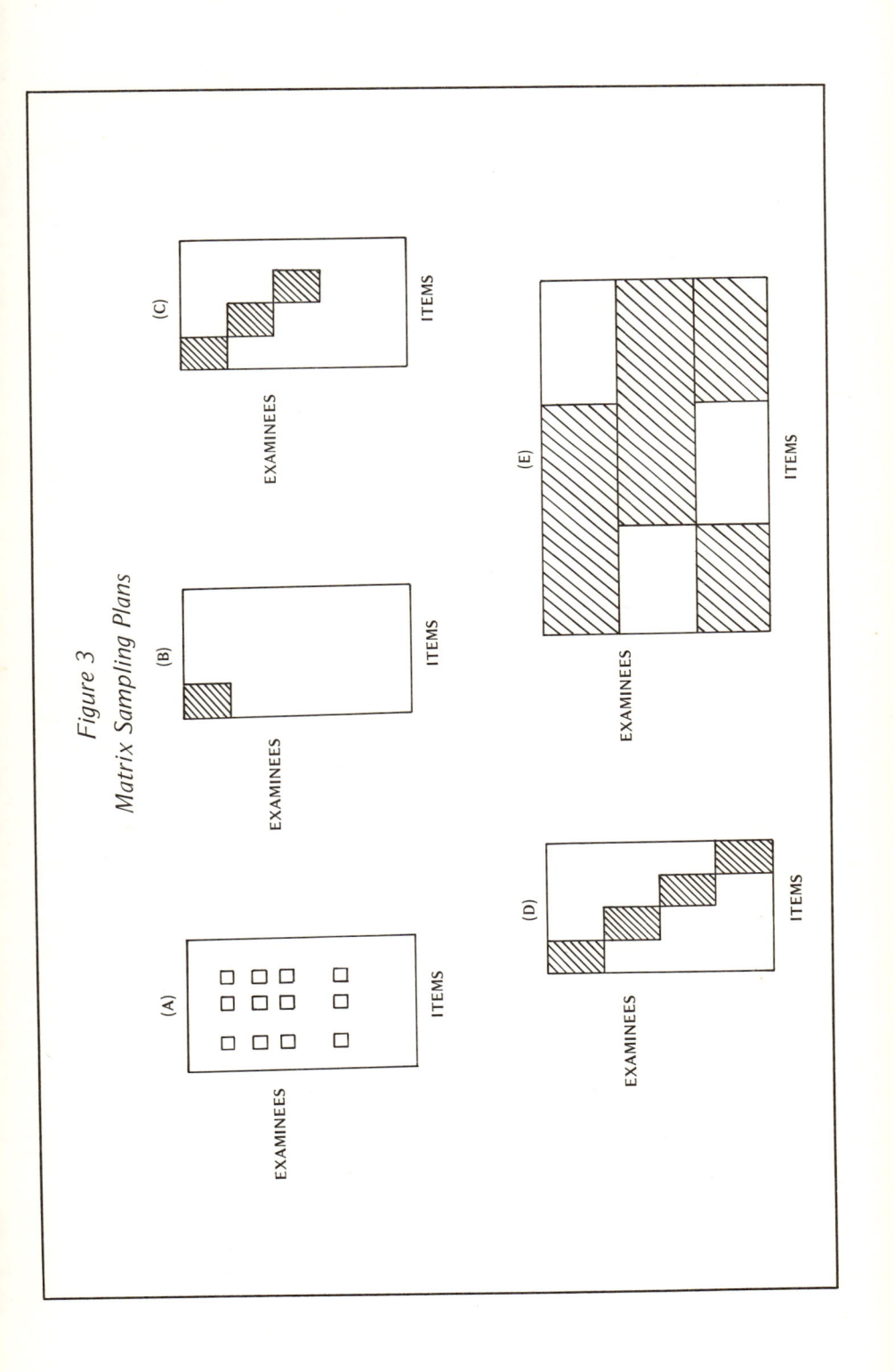

*Figure 3*
*Matrix Sampling Plans*

times the square root of this variance can be used to estimate a *UB* for the domain score.

Figure 3b is meant to illustrate the same plan as Figure 3a, namely, that a random sample of examinees is each given the same random sample of items. The four examinees and three items, however, have been placed first and cover the shaded corner.

The advantages of the design sketched in 3a and 3b over the other designs is primarily one of convenience of administration and scoring. Only a single test needs to be constructed. And it can, perhaps, be administered in a single testing situation.

Design 3c illustrates a multiple matrix sampling scheme in which nonoverlapping random samples of items are formed, and each is administered to a different (random) group of examinees. The domain score computed for the sample is an unbiased estimate of the domain score for the population. Assuming equal numbers of items on each test and equal numbers of examinees in each administration group, then Formula (11.12.3) in Lord and Novick (1968) can be used to set approximate *UB*s. Design 3d is a special case of design 3c in which all items and all examinees in the domain are randomly divided into nonoverlapping subgroups. Formula (11.12.4) in Lord and Novick (1968) is relevant in this case.

The advantage of Designs 3c and 3d over 3a and 3b is greater precision in estimation. In most cases, there is little loss in convenience. The precision comes about because more items in the domain are being sampled.

Suppose a domain consists of 36 items. Assigning 12 nonoverlapping subtests of 3 items to 120 students (each of the 12 subtests taken by 10 different examinees) will, in general, provide a better estimate of the average domain score than administering all 36 items to only 10 students. This is true even though there are 360 items responses in each case, i.e., 120 x 3 = 10 x 36 = 360. Matrix sampling can also be convenient when time is limited. Administering several short tests to many students may be preferable to a long testing session for fewer students.

Design 3e illustrates a class of assignment plans in which the same item can appear in more than one subtest. Suggestions may be found in Knapp (1968) for dealing with data when, across subtests, each item appears an equal number of times. Shoemaker (1972) has performed a

Monte Carlo study of the uncertainties associated with estimates of domain scores made from assignment plans in this class.

**General Considerations**

Sampling bias should be avoided in any assignment plan. This means that there should be a random process operating whenever items or examinees (or both) are sampled. Groups of items or examinees should not be excluded ahead of time merely because it is convenient.

To avoid a biased sample, we need to make explicit the populations of items, classrooms, students, testing conditions and other factors. This is often not a simple matter. For example, suppose a domain contains some items believed to measure skills prerequisite to the ability to answer other items. Should both types of items have an equal chance to be chosen for administration? For some purposes, performance on items tapping the "terminal" skills may be of primary interest, and the domains of items from which sampling will take place should be narrowed to them alone. Another solution would be to alter the assignment plan so as to obtain a profile in which estimates for the terminal and prerequisite domains appear separately.

We also need to sample as widely as possible from the data box (Figure 1). This means including many items or item formats and many examinees or classrooms. Try to include all areas of the item-examinee matrix in your assignment plan.

Further, the "context effect" problem deserves mention. The act of taking some items often influences the ability of examinees to pass other items. There may be practice or interference effects specifically related to particular assignment plans. If an item appears in the context of other similar items it may be easier to answer than if it appears with widely differing ones. For examinee evaluation perhaps the best advice is to keep it in mind and look for cases where the context may make a difference in your particular application. For program evaluation, context effects can by minimized by a matrix sampling plan in which many examinees are each administered only a few items.

Finally, the foregoing estimates were fundamentally derived from a model in which the number of items a person knows, or the number of people an item "knows," are each thought of as being like the number of white balls in an urn that contains an unknown black and white mixture. To utilize this model we only have to assume that the sample is randomly drawn and that the experience of taking the earlier items on a test does not influence the examinee's chance of passing the later items. No assumptions regarding item homogeneity in content or difficulty are needed. Regression and Bayesian models provide an alternate model for estimating domain scores. See, e.g., Cronbach *et al.* (1972), especially Chapter 5 and pp. 385-386, and Novick (1973).

## References

Cochran, W.G. *Sampling Techniques* (Second edition). New York: John Wiley and Sons, 1963.

Cronbach, L.J. *et al. The Dependability of Behavioral Measurements: Theory of Generalizability for Scores and Profiles.* New York: John Wiley and Sons, 1972.

Knapp, T.R. An Application of Balanced Incomplete Block Designs to the Estimation of Test Norms. *Educational and Psychological Measurement,* 1968, 28, 265-272.

Lord, F.M. and M.R. Novick. *Statistical Theories of Mental Test Scores.* Reading, Mass.: Addison-Wesley Publishing Company, 1968.

Marascuilo, L.A. *Statistical Methods for Behavioral Science Research.* New York: McGraw-Hill, 1971.

Novick, M.R. Untitled presentation given at the annual meeting of the American Educational Research Association, New Orleans, 1973.

Shoemaker, D.M. Standard Errors of Estimate in Item-Examinee Sampling as a Function of Test Reliability, Variation in Item Difficulty Indices and Degree of Skewness in the Normative Distribution. *Educational and Psychological Measurement,* 1972, 32, 705-714.

# PART TWO

# APPLICATIONS AND INNOVATIONS

# Test-Item Domains and Instructional Accountability

Donald B. Sension and
George J. Rabehl

**Pressures for Accountability**
The pressures for accountability in education are steadily mounting. Local taxpayer groups want evidence that the dollars they invest in school buildings, teaching supplies and salaries produce an adequate return. "Do more at all costs" has changed to "What really needs to be done? Who can do it best and with least expense?"

Elected officials at national, state and local levels, who must allocate resources for educational programs, are demanding accurate needs-assessment to assist in decision-making. Teachers and administrators who must decide between alternative learning packages are asking for accurate evaluative information on the many methods, materials and modes of instruction available. A final pressure for accountability comes from self-directed students searching for ways to document their individual accomplishments apart from institutionally defined goals.

**The Nature of Instructional Accountability**
*The Changing Concept of Accountability*
The roots of instructional accountability are at least as old as the

**Donald B. Sension** is with the Hopkins, Minnesota Public Schools. **George J. Rabehl** is with the Osseo, Minnesota Public Schools.

early writings of E.L. Thorndike (1904). However, its recent resurgence is often associated with the idea of performance contracting. The result has been the identification of instructional accountability with the execution of formal agreements between producer and consumer (Lessinger, 1973). We consider this to be an unnecessarily narrow use of the term "accountability." We see the concept shifting to a more comprehensive framework involving the whole school community. It is becoming apparent that an "accountable school" is one in which the whole staff is taking steps to document and satisfactorily explain the operation and outcomes of its instructional system.

*Accountability: Documenting and Presenting Information About Student-Centered Goals and Instructional Procedures*

It is useful if we make a distinction between two parts of an instructional program. First, we can identify the student-centered goals and objectives of the program, i.e., what we want to teach. Second, we can isolate the procedures that we arrange in an effort to obtain the desired learning. The correspondence of these curricular components with the now common product-process distinction is evident.

Instructional accountability is concerned with the collection and dissemination of six types of information, represented by the cells in Table 1.

*Table 1*

*Types of Accountability Information*

|  | Characteristics | Evaluation Evidence | Plans for Revision |
|---|---|---|---|
| Student Goals and Objectives | 1 | 2 | 3 |
| Instructional Procedures | 4 | 5 | 6 |

An *accountable* school describes and documents its goals and objectives (Cell 1) and the instructional procedures currently in use (Cell 4). It presents evaluative evidence concerning the worth of the objectives (Cell 2) and teaching processes used (Cell 5). Insofar as a careful evaluation will reveal weaknesses as well as strengths, the accountable school includes opportunities for revisions in each area (Cells 3 and 6). (Independent School District No. 279, 1973; and Rabehl, 1971a).

*Accountability as It Involves*
*Goals and Objectives*
Our premise is that a responsible school system should be able to describe the knowledge, skills and attitudes that it is attempting to teach its students. The descriptions may be made to fit different administrative or student grouping levels. Besides over-all school district goals, there are goals appropriate to buildings, departments and classes, as well as individual students.

The school system should not only be able to describe its goals and objectives, but it should also be able to explain their worth. Judgmental evidence includes feedback from students, parents, board members, experts in the field, employers who hire students, etc. Experimental evidence comes from studies which validate task analyses leading to terminal competence of some type: Is it really necessary to learn X before you can do Y?

The obligation of a school is not to be perfect, but rather to evaluate and revise in a continuing cycle leading to improved instruction and better confirmation of the relevance of what is taught.

*Accountability as It Involves*
*Instructional Procedures*
There are two principal reasons for describing the goal and the instructional procedures used in school programs (Cell 4 of Table 1). First, the public has a right to know and, as many school systems are finding out, wants to know what is occurring within the schools. The open education movement, for example, stems to some extent from the dissatisfaction of some parents and educators with the objectives of conventional programs, how they are established and how they are met. Advocates of open education argue that goals for self-direction and self-motivation cannot be met in the conventional classroom, where

objectives are established with little regard to the desires of individual students and where instructional procedures center around planned activities that have little connection to students' interests.

A second reason for documenting goals and instructional procedures derives from the advantage this affords curriculum developers. It is difficult to talk about projecting systematic change in the future unless the present situation is understood by all concerned.

Many indices may be examined in determining the effectiveness of administrative and classroom methods as they relate to instruction. An important index is, of course, student achievement. District, building, program, and classroom and individual assessments may be made. Other indices of the effectiveness of instructional procedures involve teacher, student and parent satisfaction. The amounts of time required for learning to occur and the costs of instructional materials are also important.

The accountable school is not expected to provide instructional procedures which at any given time are considered to be ideal from all standpoints. Improvements will always be in order. Teachers and administrators and students propose changes (Cell 6—revision) that will increase the effectiveness and desirability of the teaching procedures. These may involve such diverse changes as the introduction of new instructional materials, changes in methodology, changes in student groupings, the use of paraprofessionals or development of needed inservice programs.

The particular processes that are utilized in gathering information about the objectives and methods of an instructional program must be selected or developed to fit the situation. It would be a mistake to prescribe procedures for all instructional areas or administrative systems. Nevertheless, certain approaches seem to have promise. One of these involves the application of the principles of domain-referenced testing.

**Test Item Domains and Instructional Accountability**

*Where Domains Fit In*

*A domain, as the term is used here, is a set of test items which have explicitly defined, fundamental properties in common.* The concept of a domain thus involves a general classification scheme for items, together with a number of representative examples under each

*Domains and Instructional Accountability* 49

heading of the classification. Test-item domains are a boon to the accountable school.

First, they facilitate the specification and eventually the evaluation of objectives (Cells 1 and 2 of Table 1). We describe what we want students to learn in the classroom in terms of performances on the items in appropriate domains. Teachers can sit down with parents, administrators or other teachers and describe with considerable clarity and precision exactly what they are trying to teach.

Some curricula are based on teaching sequences in which students are expected to master tasks at certain levels before going on to the next step. Domains help in the description of these instructional procedures by clearly identifying the activities that are used at each level (Cell 4).

Domain-referenced tests are uniquely suited to the task of evaluating instructional procedures. A chronic problem in achievement testing for accountability concerns the fear that instructors will teach for the test and that results will then not fairly reflect student competence. The concern is perhaps justified when the program utilizes standardized, norm-referenced tests involving a relatively small number of items. Consequently, we hide the test from the teacher with the result that we hold a teacher responsible for teaching knowledge and skill that we have not defined. In the domain-referenced approach, the classified pools of items are made available to teachers who may teach for the whole domain. Achievement tests are prepared by sampling from the domains. If the domains adequately cover the area of interest, and if the representative pools are large, the dangers of "teaching for the test" are negligible. Indeed, "teaching for the test" may be a very desirable activity.

The implementation of a domain-referenced accountability system involves several interrelated tasks:

1. Domains must be developed and described in such a way that staff members, students, parents and interested members of the public can understand their contents.
2. Student and item sampling designs and test administration procedures which fit local resources as well as the demands of accountability must be developed.
3. Data analysis and reporting procedures which answer questions at appropriate administrative levels at opportune times must be prepared. The data needs of board members,

administrators, teachers and students differ, as do the nature and frequency of their decisions.
4. Provisions for revision must be built into the system with attention given to the implementation of changes in the short run as well as those made on a yearly basis.

## Applications in Two School Systems

Domain-referenced tests are currently being used in the implementation of accountability procedures at Hopkins, Minnesota and Osseo, Minnesota. In the 1972-1973 school year, the testing programs in these two systems served over 300 teachers and 15,000 students in the subject matter areas of mathematics, science, reading, social studies, language arts, speech and music.

Efforts to develop and implement domain-referenced achievement testing systems were stimulated by ESEA Title III grants in both school districts. Hopkins worked through its "Demonstration Evaluation Center" and "Comprehensive Achievement Monitoring" (CAM) projects. The Osseo work has been done largely through a project to develop and implement "An Accountability Model for Local Education Agencies" (Independent School District No. 279, 1972 and 1973).

### Useful Test Designs

*Individual Data.* A number of distinct basic test designs have been used with success in the two school systems. The first involves the administration of a test to an individual student based on one objective. Typically, 10 items are sampled at random from a single domain and administered to obtain an estimate of a student's competence on that particular objective. This approach is useful with carefully defined programs of instruction in which mastery levels of performance are specified for each stage in a sequence. Failure of a student to meet the criterion may result in more instruction, perhaps of an alternative form, followed by retesting on another random sample of items from the same domain. This general approach is used in the Articulation Program in Osseo. An additional feature involves the administration of items from a terminal domain at the end of each major step in the sequence of instruction. The results, graphed as in Figure 1, help to meet a motivational need of the student and provide excellent documentation of achievement to be used in evaluating the program as a whole.

The Hopkins system has utilized the Comprehensive Achievement

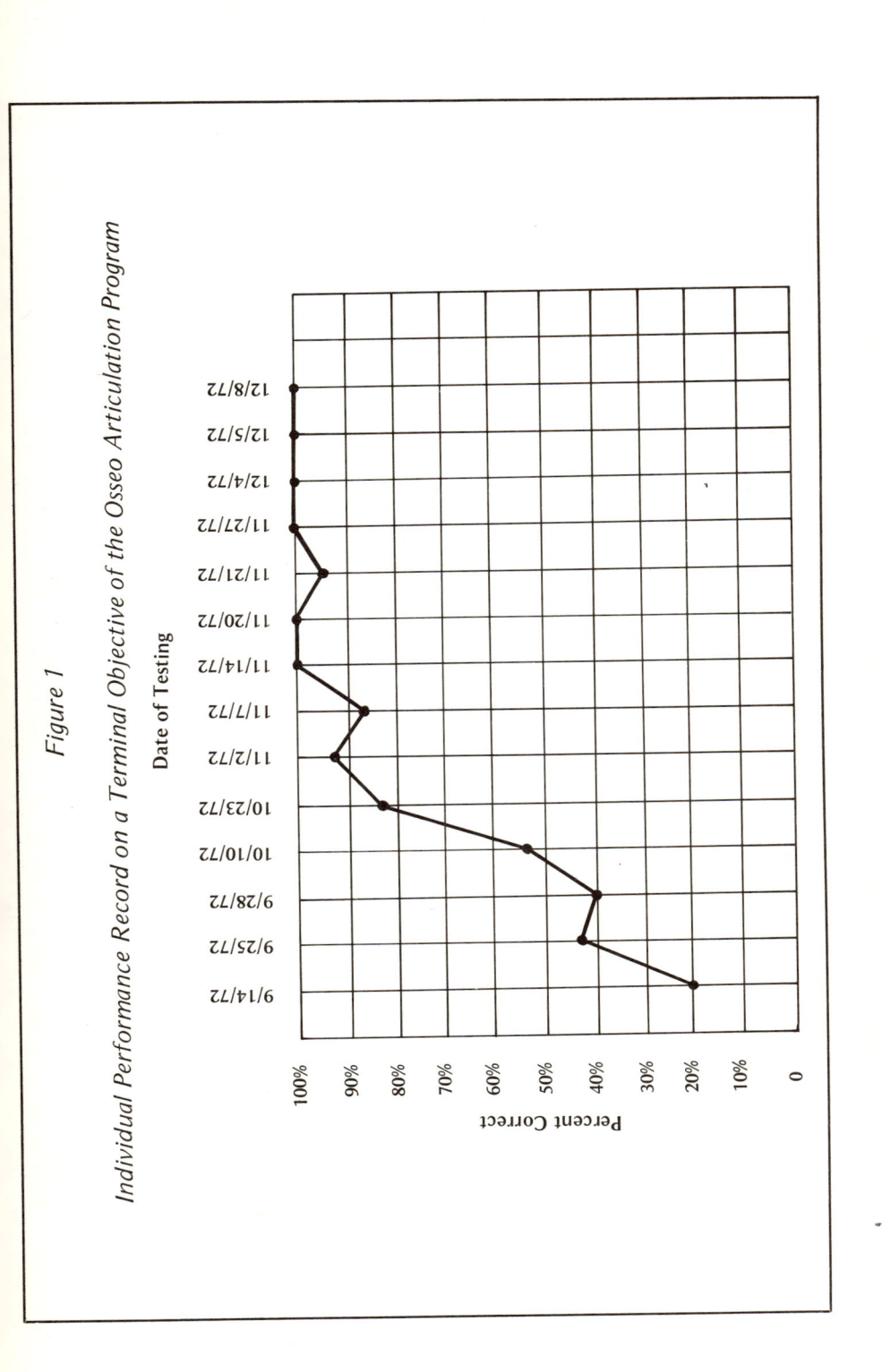

*Figure 1*

Individual Performance Record on a Terminal Objective of the Osseo Articulation Program

Monitoring (CAM) program extensively in implementing domain-referenced achievement testing on an individual basis in the regular classroom. The CAM system facilitates the collection, summarization and dissemination of pre-, post-, and retention test data. Feedback of information to teachers and students often takes the form of cumulative records similar to the one shown in Figure 2. Domain code numbers appear at the left and testing dates are across the top. An index to the code numbers is kept by the teacher and made available to students.

Students insert pluses and minuses in the record which indicate correct and incorrect responses, respectively. A blank shows that an item from that objective was not given on the occasion indicated. In consultation with his teacher, the student can use his cumulative record to decide what to review and what to tackle next. This type of data analysis obtains its power from its longitudinal nature. Normally, only one item is sampled from a domain class. Reliability of an objective score at any one testing depends to a certain degree on the homogeneity of the particular domain used. Confidence in results is thus confirmed on several testings.

*Group Data.* Useful data from domain-referenced achievement tests have also been collected and summarized on a group basis. At Osseo, for example, random samples of items from each of the 134 computation domains were given to students from each grade in elementary schools. Matrix sampling plans were used, in which not every student had the same items. This made it difficult to compare students, but the larger samples obtained from each domain made it possible to obtain fairly accurate estimates of group performance on each objective (see Millman's chapter).

Figure 3 shows the proportion of children in each grade who were able to do particular kinds of arithmetic problems at one school in November. Line No. 1 shows composite scores on four kinds of basic facts; line No. 2 shows the results on items involving the subtraction of a one-place subtrahend from a three-place minuend with repeated regrouping; line No. 3 shows the scores on items involving long division of a three-place dividend by a two-place divisor with remainder possible.

The approach has been to pinpoint the competencies of students in each grade across the 134 domain skill areas and then ask the following questions:

## Figure 2

## Student Response Grid

| Objective | Sept. 15 | Oct. 1 | Oct. 15 | Nov. 1 | Nov. 15 | Dec. 1 | Dec. 15 | Jan. 15 | Feb. 1 | Feb. 15 | Mar. 1 | | | |
|---|---|---|---|---|---|---|---|---|---|---|---|---|---|---|
| 101 | + | + | + |   |   |   | + | . | . | . | . | . | . | . |
| 102 | − | + |   |   | − | + |   | . | . | . | . | . | . | . |
| 103 |   | − | − | + | + |   | + | . | . | . | . | . | . | . |
| 201 | − |   | − | − | + | − | + | + | . | . | . | . | . | . |
| 202 | + | + | + | + | + |   | + | . | . | . | . | . | . | . |
| 203 | − | − | − | − | − | − | − | − | . | . | . | . | . | . |
| 205 | − | − | − | − | − | − | − | − | . | . | . | . | . | . |
| 310 | + | . | + | + | + | + | + | . | . | . | . | . | . | . |
| 315 | + | + | + | − | + |   | + | . | . | . | . | . | . | . |
| 320 |   | − | − | + | + | − | + | . | . | . | . | . | . | . |
| . | . | . | . | . | . | . | . | . | . | . | . | . | . | . |
| . | . | . | . | . | . | . | . | . | . | . | . | . | . | . |
| . | . | . | . | . | . | . | . | . | . | . | . | . | . | . |
| TOTAL |   |   |   |   |   |   |   |   |   |   |   |   |   |   |

KEY  + = correct response
     − = incorrect response
     Blank = objective not tested

## Figure 3

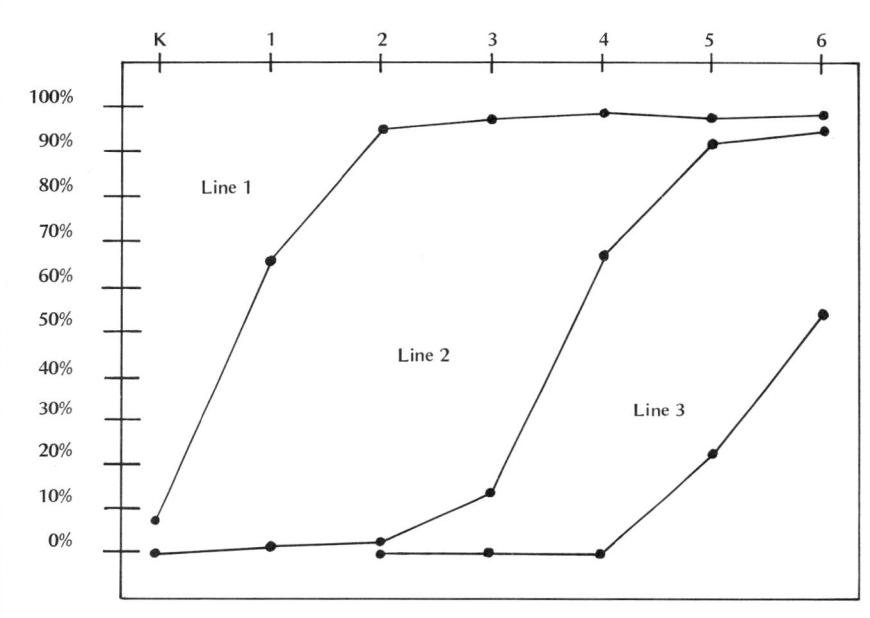

Proportion of students in each grade at Crestview Elementary School (Osseo) who could do problems of certain kinds in November, 1972.

Line 1—Basic addition facts

$$\begin{array}{r} 2 \\ +2 \\ \hline \end{array}$$

Line 2—Subtraction of a 1-place subtrahend from a 3-place minuend with repeated regrouping:

$$\begin{array}{r} 633 \\ -\phantom{0}7 \\ \hline \end{array}$$

Line 3—Long division of a 3-place dividend by a 2-place divisor with a remainder possible:

$$11 \overline{)105}$$

1. Are all entering competencies as low as expected, i.e., is it necessary to include the skill in the curriculum of a certain grade level?
2. Are all terminal competencies (sixth grade) as high as desired?
3. Are the skills being learned in the proper order?
4. What particular skills should receive priority given limited resources for program revision and curriculum change?

Profiles No. 1 and No. 2 show rather complete group mastery in two respective areas of addition and subtraction with differences due apparently to the time that the two skills were introduced and practiced. Instruction in long division of the type shown here occurs primarily in the fifth and sixth grades. Failure of scores to increase substantially could indicate a need for increased emphasis on that part of the program.

Domain-referenced testing of this type has given teachers highly specific information about the achievement of their students as a group. It helps a school faculty to evaluate priorities and plan program revisions when combined with other information about student needs.

*Domain Development and Storage*

Item forms are being used in domain development and storage, particularly at Osseo. A useful approach in both systems has been to type generated or composed items onto file cards, which are coded and stored in central item banks within sections devoted to course related or subject matter related topics. See Figure 4.

A teacher or other staff person may call for a test having certain kinds of items. A clerk goes to the file (or item form), assembles the test and sends one or more copies to the requester. The test may be saved and duplicated for others who have the same needs or new ones may be developed as the situation requires. None of this, of course, precludes the maintenance of test-item domains by individual teachers.

Domains have been developed largely by committees of teachers and resource persons in target subject matter areas with the technical assistance of evaluators in each school system, who drew heavily on techniques developed by Hively and his associates at the University of Minnesota School Mathematics and Science Teaching Project. (See Hively, Maxwell, Rabehl, Sension, and Lundin, 1973; Rabehl, 1971b; Rabehl, Jan. 24, 1972a; Rabehl, Jan. 24, 1972b.)

*56*  Domain-Referenced Testing

*Figure 4*

*Sample Item Card*

---

Which of the following facts is most relevant to this situation? "John J. Jones is now unemployed, and has been on relief for 2 years, even though he is actively seeking work."

A. Unemployment is a big problem in the trucking industry.
B. John Jones has been fired for drinking on the job by six different employers.
C. John Jones has a high school education.
D. Federal government relief programs have risen by 50 percent over the past five years.

612        0002-1              B

---

*Where Should We Begin?*

When a school district decides to move toward a domain-referenced evaluation system, several problems must be solved. The first is deciding where to begin.

Traditionally one would start from scratch by defining, evaluating and revising a whole new set of student goals and objectives (cell 1 of Table 1). In theory at least, teachers, students, parents, counselors and other interested individuals ought to be able to negotiate and define goals and objectives for students. The next step would involve describing and evaluating instructional procedures.

The development of goals and objectives in a way which is completely independent of instructional procedures may be, however, an unnecessarily idealistic approach. In some cases the development of objectives is most easily accomplished through analysis of things that teachers presently do and have their children do in the classroom (Cell 4 of Table 1). As teachers begin to examine instructional programs, the "why do this" question leads to statements of goals and objectives.

# Domains and Instructional Accountability

*How Soon Can Data Be Collected?*

The development of a domain-referenced accountability system is an evolutionary process. One begins with roughly stated goals and objectives and moves gradually toward more precisely defined domains. The need for completeness and specificity in the definition of educational objectives depends on the use for which the evaluation data are collected. If, for example, the data are to be used by teaching teams to improve the instructional process and to communicate in a general way the effectiveness of a particular course, then a few example items from each domain class may be enough to begin using the system.

**Some Things to Think About**

*The Significance of Revision in Instructional Accountability*

The importance of the third column in Table 1 cannot be overemphasized. Here we acknowledge that our objectives will, over time, be found wanting and that our instructional procedures likewise will have weaknesses. We do not expect to be held responsible for perfection, but we do expect to be held responsible for continuously defining, evaluating and improving the relevance of taught behaviors and the effectiveness of instructional procedures.

*What Does This Have to Do with Staff Evaluation?*

Instructional accountability is concerned with the collection of evidence about educational objectives and instructional procedures. Staff evaluation is a separate issue. Different school systems could apply the accountability model outlined above while at the same time retaining entirely different staff evaluation and incentive plans. By emphasizing curriculum evaluation rather than person evaluation, the present accountability model leads to greater objectivity and less tendency for persons responsible for particular areas to defend approaches that are not appropriate. Here the intent is to fire the policy—not the staff member.

This is not to deny that staff evaluation is important nor that it can be closely tied to instructional accountability. Criteria for evaluating teachers and administrators may involve the extent to which they describe, evaluate and revise instructional programs as well as the manner in which they execute existing plans. This, of course, involves a much broader definition of competence than simply the ability to maintain a certain grade-level performance as measured by standardized tests or by the achievement of externally determined objectives.

### How Difficult Is Domain-Referenced Curriculum Evaluation?

Analytical procedures and the technology of item-form writing have advanced to the point where test-item domains containing thousands of separate items can be conveniently handled. The fact remains, however, that the process takes time to learn and implement. A thorough knowledge of the subject matter of interest is necessary to the domain developer. Also important are the desire and willingness of the analyst to really come to grips with what it is that is being taught. The analyst becomes a scientist in that he tries to define the psychological variables that make a difference in teaching and learning. These become the characteristics that differentiate the classes of items in the domain—the groups of behaviors that must be treated independently in teaching and testing. The job requires training; however, teachers and school staff members have learned to do it without great difficulty.

### Can Domains Be Dangerous?

The objectives of the public school are broad and diverse. Teachers express the fear, and rightly so, that an accountability system that stresses subject matter areas which are easily analyzed will create a curriculum development process with tunnel vision. Instruction may tend to emphasize what is easily defined and assessed, to the exclusion of other important goals.

Domains are very satisfying. They facilitate communication, selection and preparation of instructional materials, and development of instruments for measuring achievement. The effort involved in their construction generally implies a good deal of personal investment by the staff members. But domains go out of date. However, because of the comfort afforded teachers in working toward familiar objectives, and because the work involved in developing new domains is considerable, work on needed curriculum revisions may languish. The potential result may be a conservative curriculum development process, and a highly refined, domain-referenced instructional system that no longer meets students' needs.

This concern, and the very real danger that it reflects, emphasizes the importance of Cell 2 in Table 1, which stresses the process of evaluating the goals and objectives on the instructional program. If we are really accountable, we should be able to present lucid arguments, backed up by concrete evidence when possible, that our objectives as described really make contemporary sense. Our obligations under the evaluative processes in Cell 5 are to show that the achievement tests we use are directly tied to the objectives of the program.

*Is Domain-Referenced Accountability an All-or-Nothing Proposition?*

The precision and clarity with which one can specify behavioral objectives and evaluate instructional procedures speaks well for a domain-referenced approach in instructional accountability. Yet we have to realize that there are other useful approaches to describing and evaluating instructional objectives and teaching procedures. The accountable teacher or administrator should be able to communicate as best he can what he is attempting to teach, why and how well, no matter where he is along the curriculum development continuum. This may mean the drafting of general objectives with two or three representative items for use in illustrating and testing for achievement. This is seen as perhaps a first step but a big one nevertheless.

Some subject matter areas are better understood than others and are thus more easily cast in a domain-referenced framework. Some behaviors involve written stimuli and written responses. These are mechanically easier to handle than, say, scientific behaviors which require the construction of apparatus to be used by students. The school system that embarks on a full-blown accountability program will thus find itself operating at different levels of specificity and precision, with the domain approach used first in the areas where it seems easiest. Other subject matter areas may follow as time and resources permit.

*Technological Problems*

The magnitude of the clerical task encountered in administering a domain-referenced testing system is almost overwhelming if the subject matter areas are broad and the domains are used to their fullest potential. A computerized central storage system is clearly needed. With such a system, every teacher can have immediate access to the item pools and be able to receive printouts of items sampled according to whatever specifications he requests.

*Who Will Do the Work?*
Persons with somewhat varied backgrounds and skills are needed for the development of viable test-item domains. Subject matter experts are needed for their command of the discipline. Teachers are needed for their understanding of the task characteristics which influence learning. Psychologists and statisticians are useful for the help they can give in validating the behavior classes defined. Behavioral systematists are needed for their taxonomic skills and their understanding of the relationships among behaviors in different subject matter areas. It is tempting to consider the development of test-item domains on a state or national basis. It appears, however, that for the immediate future, domain development is going to rest heavily on the schools that use it. Perhaps, for the sake of diversity, it always should.

*Is Domain-Referenced Accountability Worth It?*
When one observes the amount of effort that goes into a well-developed domain and the computerized sophistication required of a good achievement monitoring system, one begins to question the worth of the payoff. The answer to the above question is not an unqualified yes or no. It depends on a number of factors.

First, let us re-emphasize that not all of a curriculum needs to be nor perhaps should be defined and evaluated by using domain-referenced procedures. Where you start depends on the judged importance of the subject matter, its stability over time, the interests and competencies of available staff and the availability of published resource materials. There is probably a greater return to a school system as a whole if early resources are put into the development of domains in rather stable goal areas such as reading, math, science and social studies which involve relatively well-understood subject matter areas which have long been judged to be appropriate to the needs of many students. This is not to deny the value of a domain-referenced curriculum in more specialized course areas, some of which, such as music, lend themselves particularly well to analysis.

The logical analysis inherent in the development of a domain invariably leads to a better understanding of what competence in that subject matter is all about. Teacher growth is almost a certainty when domains are homemade. The insights gained invariably lead to revisions of present programs and a new perspective from which to judge the adequacy of published materials.

All of this, however, is premised on the assumption that the people responsible for developing and implementing instructional programs are willing to question what they did in the past and are willing to change where change appears useful. A philosophy of accountability which encourages objective self-evaluation and change rather than one which forces school personnel to defend past policies for the sake of salary and advancement is helpful, to say the least.

In answer to the question above—yes, it is worth it. Worth it if careful planning goes into the selection of the areas for development. Worth it if payoff is measured not only in terms of being able to document learning, but also in terms of the enrichment it affords participating teachers. Worth it if we consider the insights that it can provide to curriculum developers and persons responsible for the selection of instructional materials. Worth it if the school system is oriented toward change.

## References

Hively, W., M.G. Maxwell, G.J. Rabehl, D.B. Sension and S. Lundin. *Domain-Referenced Curriculum Evaluation: A Technical Handbook and a Case Study*. CSE Monograph Series in Evaluation. Los Angeles: Center for the Study of Evaluation, 1973.

Independent School District No. 279. An Overview of the District 279 Accountability Project. In District No. 279 *Educator*, April 1972.

Independent School District No. 279. Accountability Case Histories. In District No. 279 *Educator*, April 1973.

Lessinger, L. Engineering Accountability for Results in Public Education. *Phi Delta Kappan*, December 1973, 217-225.

Rabehl, G.J. Methodological Characteristics of Instructional Accountability at Osseo. Unpublished paper (available from Osseo, Minn. Public Schools), October 29, 1971a.

Rabehl, G.J. The Experimental Analysis of Educational Objectives. Doctoral Dissertation, University of Minnesota, 1971b.

Rabehl, G.J. An Item Form System. Unpublished paper (available from Osseo, Minn. Public Schools), January 24, 1972a.

Rabehl, G.J. Developing a Domain. Unpublished paper (available from Osseo, Minn. Public Schools), January 24, 1972b.

Sension, D.B. A Comparison of Two Conceptual Frameworks for Teaching the Basic Concepts of Rational Numbers. Doctoral Dissertation, University of Minnesota, 1971.

Thorndike, E.L. *An Introduction to the Theory of Mental and Social Measurement.* New York: Science Press, 1904.

## Content, Items, Decisions: Orienting Curriculum-Assessment Surveys to Curriculum Management and Modification

Donald M. Miller

What kind of empirical information about student achievement is most useful for curriculum management and modification? From my viewpoint, information for this purpose can best be obtained from curriculum-assessment surveys which (a) use instruments that correspond to specified curriculum-management plans and (b) produce indices of achievement for groups of students, not for individuals. I would like to discuss certain concepts and procedures that facilitate the construction of such survey instruments and that guide our inferences from them. Establishing correspondence of test items to curricula is the main way one demonstrates the content validity of an achievement measure. It is essential if one is to make valid inferences about management and modification of curricula. The term "achievement"

---

The topics discussed in this chapter are based on experience advising the Department of Educational Research, Ministry of Education, Venezuela. The author participated in the advisory services which were provided for the development and implementation of a national curriculum assessment survey program. He gratefully acknowledges the influence of the following advisory colleagues on the ideas presented in this chapter: Robert E. Clasen, Robert F. Conry, David E. Wiley and Richard G. Wolfe. The particular formulations described

**Donald M. Miller** is with the Ford Foundation.

refers to that which a student learns "from exposure to instruction" (Anderson, 1972). The content of instruction is specified by a curriculum management plan. Traditionally the plan specification is provided by a curriculum guide but, in general, any systematic collection of documents which sufficiently specifies curriculum content, and its organization for classroom implementation, can be considered a curriculum management plan.

The term curriculum-assessment survey refers to the procedure for obtaining census-like information about the relative incidence, distribution and interrelations of student achievement measures and curriculum/school conditions on a system-wide basis.* The intent in an assessment survey is to be both comprehensive and detailed in coverage. Since their goal is measurement of student group performance, curriculum assessment surveys typically involve simultaneous sampling of students and items in a matrix-sampling design (Husek and Sirotnik, 1967; and see Jason Millman's chapter).

## Measurement/Curriculum Correspondence:
### A Perspective

Correspondence between survey instrument and curriculum plan is essential for establishing the validity of inferences from response summaries. Lack of correspondence means that data interpretations are speculative; that no systematic links can be operationally described between the response measures and curriculum actions and decisions; and that no basis is established for formulating conclusions about the effects of a curriculum or suggesting possible modifications of its content.

Instrument correspondence means that there is an operationally specified and documented linkage between the substance and the

---

are solely those of the author and do not reflect in any way the policy or actions of the Ministry of Education, nor do they reflect the interests and policies of the Ford Foundation. The presentation is viewed as an opportunity to discuss certain issues and problems, and it is with this understanding that Ramon Pinango, Director of the Department of Educational Research, permitted its preparation. Official papers describing the curriculum assessment research in Venezuela are listed in the references.

*Kerlinger (1967) provides a concise discussion of the goals and methods of scientific surveys in educational research.

## Curriculum-Assessment Surveys

structure of the survey instrument and that of the curriculum plan. In the paradigm that has guided the advisory work on the assessment surveys in Venezuela, the survey instrument is based on the curriculum management plan and *not* on the curriculum to which students are actually exposed in the classroom.* The limitations of this paradigm are highlighted in Figure 1. The solid-lined boxes and their interconnections indicate the substantive and structural relationships which can be operationally specified and documented to be in correspondence, and which are directly treated by survey summaries; the curriculum plan, the survey instrument and the data summaries are correspondent in substance and structure. The broken-lined boxes and their interconnections indicate the linkage for which there is no direct observation in an assessment survey: no direct information is collected concerning the correspondence of classroom activities or student learning to the planned curriculum. (Such information can be gathered, but it is an expensive undertaking.)

The correspondence of achievement measures to curriculum content is a methodological criterion generally accepted by the educational research community. It is considered an essential aspect of establishing the content validity of a measuring instrument. Typical of textbook discussions on educational measurement, Thorndike and Hagen (1969) recommend that "...we must match the analysis of test content against the analysis of course content and instructional objectives and see how well the former represents the latter.... Test content is drawn from what has been taught, or proposed to be taught. The instructional program is the original source material."

Yet despite these generally accepted ideas, rarely do studies on student achievement and its relation to curriculum/school conditions talk about the correspondence between measurement instrument and curriculum content. Even rarer is the effort to report procedures by which correspondence was attempted. Rarest of all is the effort to operationally specify and document the actual measurement/curriculum correspondence. Recently, Anderson (1972) presented a survey of reported practices by investigators using achievement measuring instruments. He found that "Most investigators reported nothing about their tests beyond such rudimentary information as the number of items and

---

*See the references for official documents describing the Venezuela National Assessment Program.

*Figure 1*

The Limits of Direct Inferences: A Paradigm

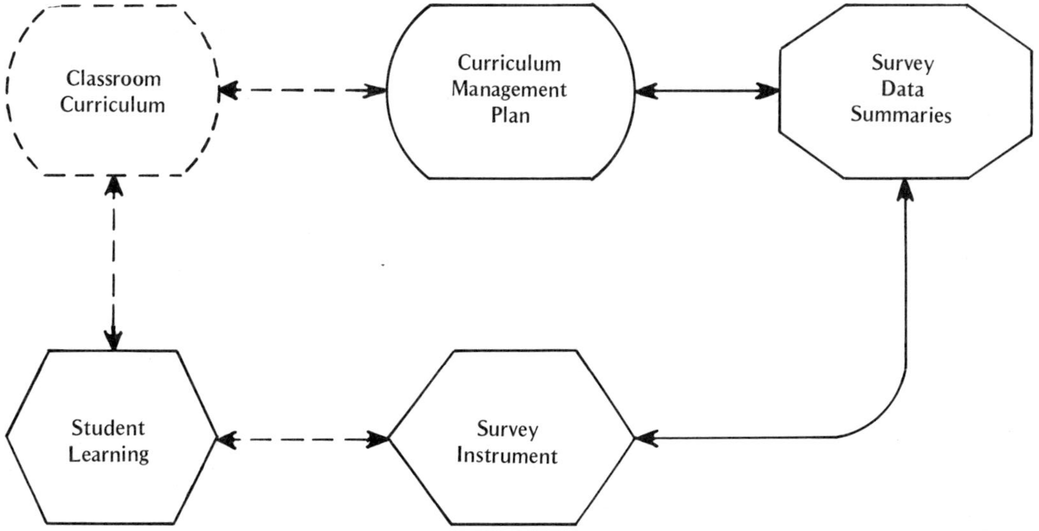

the response mode." Approximately 51 percent of the reports failed to provide any information about the relation of test items to instruction and the other 49 percent provided only limited information. For example, 14 percent provided sufficient information for Anderson to conclude that their "items clearly measured verbatim recognition and recall" of the instructional material.

Unfortunately, frequent use is made of norm-referenced, standardized achievement or ability measures for examining the relationship between curriculum/school resources and student achievement. It is unfortunate because, although norm-based tests often begin with a domain of content approximating a curriculum, the nature of normative test construction ultimately leads to a distortion, or lack of correspondence, between the test and the content area originally specified. Cox (1965) observed such lack of correspondence between instructional objectives and selected items. An example of such distortion will be given below, based on a set of assessment survey items in mathematics.

## Establishing Correspondence:
## An Outline of Procedures

The goal of a curriculum assessment survey is to obtain information on student achievement explicated in terms of the substance and structure of the curriculum. Summaries of student achievement within this framework provide a basis for formulating inferences about the management of the curriculum, for suggesting possible modifications to the curriculum and for setting realistic expectations of student achievement. To accomplish these goals, a correspondence must be established between the measures and the curriculum, and this correspondence must be operationally specified and documented. The discussion which follows outlines a set of procedures.

### A Paradigm for Measurement/
### Curriculum Correspondence

Seven major procedures must be undertaken: (1) curriculum management plan documentation, (2) survey design specification, (3) content domain specification, (4) content decomposition and transformation to test items, (5) item pool assembly, (6) survey instrument specification and (7) data summarization. A paradigm of these procedures is given in Figure 2. Activities A, B and C are concerned

*Figure 2*

Measurement/Curriculum Correspondence:
A Paradigm of Procedures

A. Curriculum Management Plan Documentation → B. Survey Design Specification → C. Content Domain Definition

D. Decomposition and Transformation of Content

E. Item Pool Assembly → F. Survey Instrument Specification → G. Data Summarization

Formation of Inferences

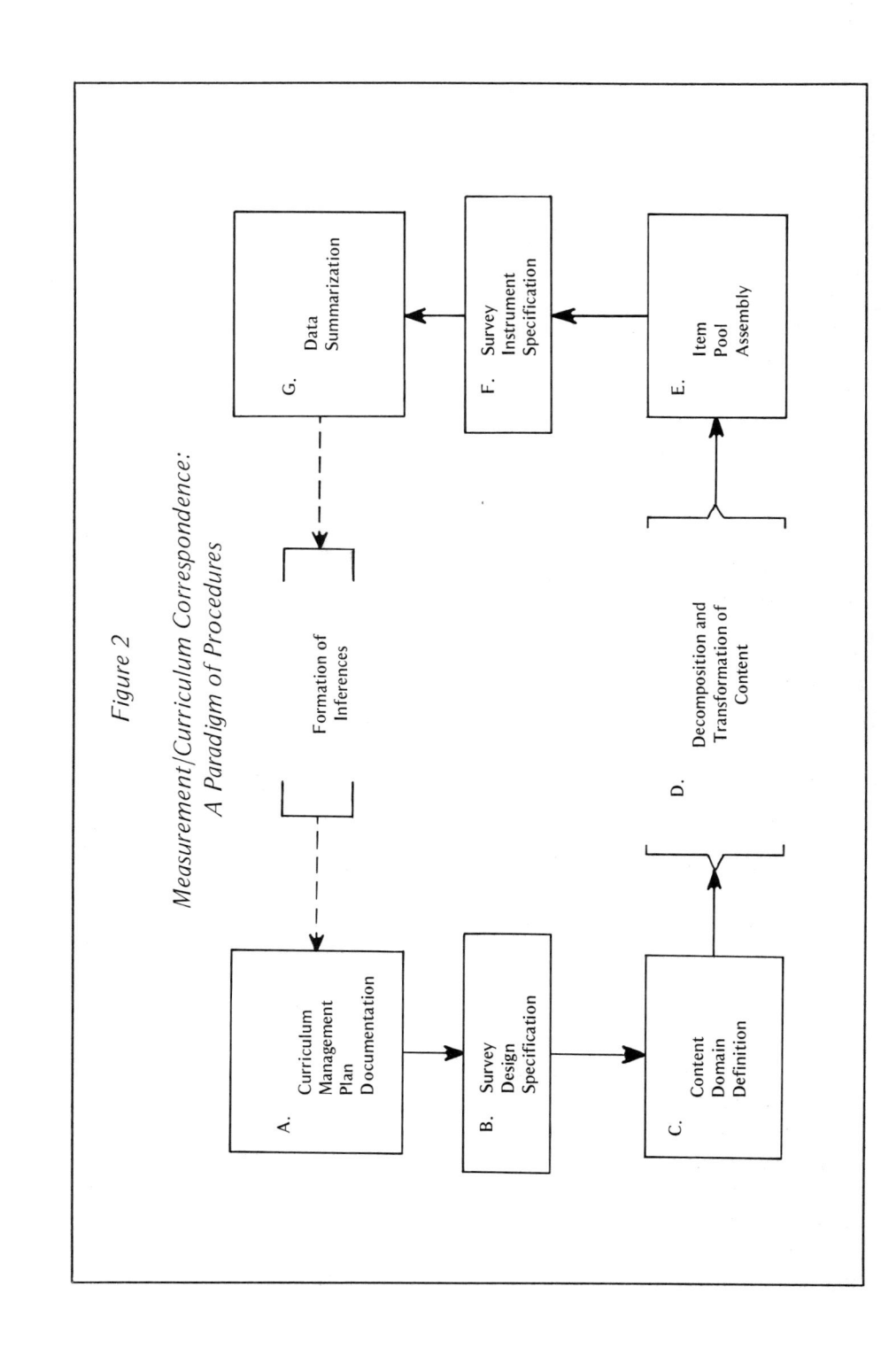

*Curriculum-Assessment Surveys* 69

with the explication of curriculum content. The documentation of the management plan provides the basis for delimiting the exact content dimensions of the survey. These dimensions should include both the logical classification structure of the subject matter and the organizational management plan for curriculum implementation (e.g., the sequence in which concepts are taught). The selected content dimensions, together with the target population of students to be surveyed, form basic parameters of the survey design (Activity B). In Activity C an exact definition is prepared of the content domain; this is composed of the substantive material and an explication of the structural characteristics. This documentation should be augmented during the item construction work if additional materials are consulted as sources of item content.

Activity D involves a series of tasks by which curriculum content is decomposed and transformed into test items. This work begins with the content domain definition and ends with item production. The origins of every item must be traceable to their source in the content domain. The traceability of items is critical for two reasons: (1) it is essential evidence for substantive equivalence of the survey instrument, and (2) various reports will present data summaries for items together with inferences about their relationship to the corresponding parts of the curriculum management plan. (The process of decomposition and transformation is discussed in the next section of this chapter.)

The assembly of the item pool, Activity E, involves a formal evaluation of the item traceability records and the structural character of the pool. Checking traceability, and reporting its reliability, is essential for evidencing correspondence. The organization of items at this phase, and their archiving, should be in accord with the category of taxonomic structure defined by the content domain in Activity C.* It is critical that the codification of items be completed and evaluated.

Tabulations should be made of items according to their structural classifications. The distribution of items across categories should be equivalent to the content distribution across the structural features of the content domain. How this can be done may be unclear until some

---

*This does not imply that the archive organization and procedures should be operationally defined in these terms. For example, the items can be filed according to some accession number and their codes used to generate permuted indexes which permit rapid location of any item.

experience is gained in using various indicators (e.g., number of class hours); one strategy is to base the distribution of items on the proportional character of the content units defined by the decomposition procedures in Activity A.

The documentation and archiving of the item pool accomplished in Activity E provides the basis for final specification of the survey instrument (Activity F). The general parameters of instrument design will depend on the availability of resources for the conduct of the survey and its analysis and reporting (particularly the time limitations within which the survey must be completed). In a situation of very limited resources or severe time limits, a decision might be made at this stage to reduce the size of the survey: for example, if the original domain specifications were for fundamental operations in sixth grade mathematics, then the survey might be reduced to an assessment of only subtraction and division. Proportional sampling of items can be utilized using matrix-sampling techniques to reduce the number of items in the final survey instrument.

After the field operations and data reductions have been completed, various summaries of student responses can be prepared (Activity G). The simplest is to calculate the percentage of students responding correctly to each item. Composite summaries can be prepared according to the structural specifications of the domain. For example, in a survey of sixth grade mathematics, separate summaries might be prepared for subtraction with integers, subtraction with decimals, etc.; and a composite index might be prepared for subtraction in general. Such summaries can be prepared in combination with the various classifications of students, following the design specifications. At present, techniques for accomplishing these various kinds of summaries, especially composite summaries, are underdeveloped.

*Content Decomposition and Transformation*

The decomposition of content defined by the domain specification, and its transformation into survey items, is accomplished by a series of activities divided into two phases: Phase A is the specification and codification of the taxonomic structure of the content; Phase B is the construction of the items. A procedural algorithm is outlined in Figure 3.

The goal of Phase A, Content Taxonomy Specification, is the structural decomposition of the content domain into its smallest

*Figure 3*

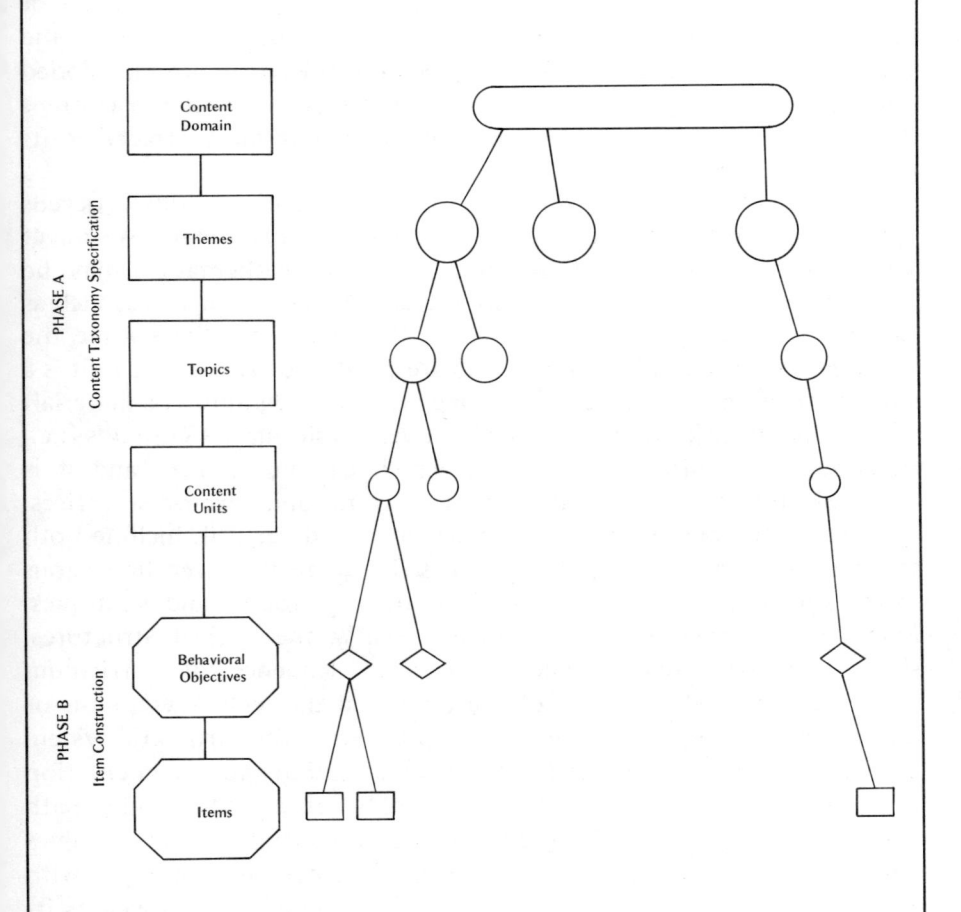

*Content Decomposition and Transformation:
A Paradigm Using Traditional Procedures*

entities, labeled content units. The result of this work is an inventory of content units organized according to the content taxonomy.

The taxonomic features of the domain are explicated by a process of "anatomical" separation, or disassembly, without any modification of their substantive character. This explication should be completely reversible. That is, the array of content units can be jig-sawed or reassembled, exactly reproducing the content domain. During the process of structural decomposition, the separated structures are coded and documented in detail so that the reproducibility of the content domain can be established and each content unit can be traced to its original location in the domain.

The exact manner in which this structural decomposition proceeds will depend on the nature of the particular content domain. A subject with a precise logic to its structure, such as mathematics, may be decomposed with greater precision and speed than other areas, such as history or civics. In general, however, the goal is to disassemble the domain structure until content units are produced. A content unit is a statement (perhaps with accompanying visual or diagrammatic material) which has intrinsic unity, it is substantively molecular, it contains (i.e., describes, or expresses) something which can be learned, and it is amenable for transformation into a behavioral objective or objectives.

The taxonomic dimensions, horizontal and vertical, include both subject matter and management factors. The subject matter dimensions might hierarchically disassemble into themes, topics and subtopics. Management dimensions will usually qualify the subject structures, since they will indicate such factors as sequence of curriculum implementation, the density of the topic and the relative emphasis of one topic with respect to the other topics. Since this structural system can be complex, detailed and accurate codification and documentation is essential. For example, the disassembly of a sixth grade math curriculum might identify the fundamental operations, then topics defined by the four kinds of numbers, then codify each topic with respect to its sequential position in the curriculum plan as well as its degree of emphasis with respect to the other topics.

The goal of Phase B, Item Construction, is the transformation of the content units into response items. The result is an inventory of items organized according to the structural taxonomy produced in Phase A. The transformations are coded and documented so that each item can be traced to its originating content unit. Consequently, the items or item pool is substantively and structurally equivalent to the content unit inventory and to the content domain.

It is essential, whatever method of transformation (i.e., item writing) is used, that the procedure be sufficiently specified and documented to permit replication.* Cronbach (1971) has suggested that a duplicate-construction experiment would be a desirable way of investigating the content validity of these kinds of tests or survey instruments. This specification should include description of any training or orientation provided to the individuals who actually perform the decomposition and transformation; for example, classroom teachers might be trained according to standard procedures which can be replicated with several groups.

A traditional approach to item writing which might be applied in Phase B is that of transforming content units into behavioral objectives and the objectives into items. This approach is comprehensively treated by Bloom, Hastings and Madaus (1971). Instructional objectives would be derived from the content units by explication of the content components and the behavioral components (the content components in the present algorithm were specified in Phase A). Then the objectives would be classified in a two-dimensional table of specifications defined by the content classification and a classification of behaviors.

Another method of item-writing, proposed by Bormuth (1971), promises to provide measures which have high degrees of substantive and structural equivalence between measuring instrument and curriculum content domain. Bormuth presents a theory of achievement test construction based on linguistic analysis. He emphasizes the critical importance of procedural specification and replicability.

Within the perspective of the present paradigm, whatever method of item writing is applied, the final procedure should be revision and editing of the items. This procedure should follow logical guidelines based on the procedural specifications designed to ensure substantive

---

*Circumstances permitting, replication should actually be made, perhaps of only a selected portion of the content if research resources are limited. The result of the replication would be a second inventory of items which should approximate the original inventory in terms of substance and structure. The overlap between these inventories should be determined. A satisfactory degree of overlap might be 75 percent. If the overlap is too small, then a very detailed review of operations and their documentation should be made in an effort to improve specification to establish replicability.

and structural equivalence of the instrument to the curriculum management plan.

In summary, this section has outlined concepts and procedures for constructing a survey instrument which closely corresponds to the curriculum management plan. Correspondence has been defined in terms of the substantive and structural equivalence of the instrument to the curriculum plan. The substantive equivalence is specified by the operational definition of the content domain and the documentation of item traceability by which each item is demonstrably linked through the various stages of decomposition and transformation to its originating content location in the content domain. Structural equivalence is evidenced by documentation of the taxonomic equivalence of the survey instrument to the content domain and insuring that the proportional distribution of items across the taxonomic categories is the same as the distribution of content across the specified taxonomic structure.

*Selected Illustrations*

Three concepts outlined in the procedures described above will be illustrated. These are (a) content decomposition and transformation, (b) the structural equivalence of an instrument and (c) data summarization. The data for these illustrations are drawn from official reports of a national assessment survey of sixth grade mathematics in Venezuela.* This survey was designed to provide empirical information on student achievement which would contribute to a review and revision of the national curriculum. Empirical information was desired which would describe the incidence, distribution and interrelationships of student achievement variables within the context of curriculum/ school conditions and resources.

*Departamento de Investigaciones Educacionales. *Conocimientos Generales de los Educandos-Sexto Grado: Matematicas y Lenguaje.* Serie I: Informes Preliminares. Direccion de Planeamiento, Ministerio de Education, Caracas, Venezuela, 1970. L. Leon, C. Mendoza and R. Pinango. *Nivel de Aprendizaje de los Estudiantes Venezolanos de Sexto Grado en Adicion, Sustraccion, Multiplicacion, Division.* Departamento de Investigaciones Educacionales. Direccion de Planeamiento, Ministerio de Educacion, Caracas, Venezuela, 1971. R. Pinango, R. Blanco and D. Miller. Educational Research and Curriculum Reform: The Case of the Venezuelan Assessment Program. Presented at the American Educational Research Association Annual Meeting, 1971.

*Illustration A—Decomposition and Transformation.* The structural derivation of a survey item is given in Table 1. By the attachment of codes, an item can be traced to its original source content in the curriculum plan. That is, the item resulted from an *objective* which was constructed from a *content unit* concerning the addition of integers in columns of five digits. This *content unit* was an entity in a section of the curriculum on the *topic* addition, which in turn can be considered to form a section of the *theme* fundamental operations.

*Illustration B—Structural Equivalence.* The 11 topic categories of the sixth grade math curriculum are listed in Table 2, together with the percentages of content units, behavioral objectives and items falling under each category. The first distribution of items shows the total pool of items which resulted from the transformation of the content units; this pool was too large for complete application in the survey. The second distribution of items is for the items actually composing the survey instrument. These were sampled in such a way as to reflect the same relative distribution as in the total pool. The third distribution of items represents a hypothetical test for which items were selected according to item-statistic criteria of the type typically used in norm-reference test construction; for this table, items were selected if (a) the correct alternative correlated + 0.30 with the total score, and (b) the distractors correlated 0.00 or negatively with the total score.

The distributions of content units and behavioral objectives may be considered indicators of the distribution of the content in the over-all domain, and so these distributions can be used as criteria against which to evaluate the structural equivalence of survey instruments. The distribution of items used in the assessment survey instrument approximately correspond to the distribution of the content units. But, the distribution for the items in the hypothetical norm-referenced test shows certain critical deviations from the content unit distribution. In the case of one category, "Proportions," normative item-selection criteria cause omittance of all items, and in the case of the "Division" category a disproportionately large number of items were included. Further, the normative item-selection criteria caused a severe reduction in the total number of items—from 321 items to 87, a 73 percent reduction in the content coverage of the instrument with respect to the content domain.

*Illustration C—Data Summarization.* A variety of data summaries have been presented in the cited reports from the Venezuela Assess-

*Table 1*

*Decomposition and Transformation:
An Example*

| PHASE A | Stage | Product |
|---|---|---|
| Content Taxonomy Specification | Subject | Mathematics in the sixth grade |
| | Theme | Fundamental Operations |
| | Topic | Addition |
| | Subtopic | Addition with whole numbers |
| | Content unit | Addition to integers in columns of five digits |

| PHASE B | | |
|---|---|---|
| Item Construction | Behavioral Objective | Given an addition problem of up to five digits the student will be able to select, from among various alternatives, the correct alternative |
| | Item | The result of the operation indicated at the left is |

```
         _____ 47,896     _____ 48,796    + 2,365
                                           45,721
         _____ 48,886     _____ 48,896        489
                                              321
                                             ____
```

Source: Departamento de Investigaciones Educacionales, 1970.

## Table 2

### Summary Information on Instrument Correspondence: An Example

Approximate Percentages of Content Units, Behavioral
Objectives and Items in Topic Categories

Subject: Sixth Grade Mathematics

| Topics | Content Units | Behavioral Objectives | Total Items Written | Assessment Survey Items | Hypothetical Norm-referenced Test |
|---|---|---|---|---|---|
| 1. Numeration | 5 | 6 | 5 | 5 | 9 |
| 2. Addition | 7 | 10 | 12 | 8 | 3 |
| 3. Subtraction | 9 | 10 | 16 | 8 | 8 |
| 4. Multiplication | 11 | 8 | 11 | 8 | 12 |
| 5. Division | 16 | 17 | 18 | 23 | 41 |
| 6. Percentage | 9 | 7 | 6 | 8 | 6 |
| 7. Interest/Discount | 7 | 5 | 6 | 4 | 3 |
| 8. Home Arithmetic | 7 | 6 | 3 | 5 | 3 |
| 9. Proportion | 5 | 4 | 2 | 5 | 0 |
| 10. Metric System | 15 | 16 | 12 | 18 | 12 |
| 11. Geometry | 9 | 11 | 9 | 8 | 3 |
| | 100% (N = 81) | 100% (N = 122) | 100% (N = 597) | 100% (N = 321) | 100% (N = 87) |

Source (partial): Departamento de Investigaciones Educacionales, 1973.

ment for various classifications of students. Some examples involving the item presented in Table 1 will illustrate the nature of data summarization possible from an assessment survey. To that item (concerning the addition of integers with five digits) approximately 89 percent of students answered correctly. Across all items involving the four fundamental operations with whole numbers, about 65 percent of the students responded correctly. For the topic, "addition" (across the four kinds of numbers—integers, decimals, fractions and mixed) 52 percent of the students answered correctly. And when both these topics were taken in combination, represented by all items involving the addition of whole numbers, the proportion of students answering correctly was 88 percent.

## Summary: Selected Comments

It has been argued that the correspondence of a measuring instrument to curriculum content is critical for curriculum management and modification, and for assessing the effect of the curriculum implementation on student learning. A particular emphasis was given to the importance of establishing measurement/curriculum correspondence in terms of operational specifications which are documented, which ensure that the measurement procedures are content valid, which permit replication, and which produce measurements of student learning which can be directly mapped to the curriculum management plan. Attention was given to some traditional measurement procedures which tend to restrict instrument correspondence. An example showed that when item selections are made according to the kinds of item statistics typically used in norm-referenced test construction a measuring instrument results which is biased with respect to the substance and structure of the content domain.

The measurements of student learning obtained from a curriculum assessment survey of this type pose several issues requiring research and development. Perhaps of prime importance are the conceptual tools and experience needed for properly interpreting the measures and assessing their implications. The difficulty in this is that very few estimates of student achievement of this kind have been obtained. What are our realistic expectations of student performance? Do we expect that 100 percent of sixth grade students will correctly answer a set of problems involving the addition of whole numbers? Or can we only expect that 65 percent of sixth graders will respond correctly? It seems to the author that experience must be gained in formulating realistic expectations of these kinds before formal criterion levels or standards can be specified. Before we can realistically domain-reference the goals of student achievement we should be able to state realistic expectations. Viable and efficient distribution of educational resources is greatly facilitated by expectations of student achievement which are realistically estimated within the limits of resources available.

## References

Anderson, R.C. How to Construct Achievement Tests to Assess Comprehension. *Review of Educational Research*, Spring 1972, Vol. 42, No. 2, 145-170.
Blanco, R.F. Item Analysis of Student Responses to a Venezuelan National Assessment Survey of the Sixth Grade Mathematics Curriculum. Seccion Estadistica, Departamento de Investigaciones Educacionales, Direccion de Planeamiento, Ministerio de Educacion. Caracas, Venezuela. Technical Memo, 1971.
Bloom, B.S., J.T. Hastings and G.F. Madaus. *Handbook on Formative and Summative Evaluation of Student Learning*. New York: McGraw-Hill, 1971.
Bormuth, J.R. *On the Theory of Achievement Test Items*. Chicago: University of Chicago Press, 1971.
Cox, R.C. Item Selection Techniques and Evaluation of Instructional Objectives. *J. of Educ. Measurement*, December 1965, *2* (2).
Cronbach, L.J. Test Validation. Chapter 14 in R.L. Thorndike (Ed.) *Educational Measurement* (Second Edition). Washington, D.C.: American Council on Education, 1971.
Departamento de Investigaciones Educacionales. Propositos, Situacion Actual y Programas de Actividales del Departamento de Investigaciones Educacionales. *Educacion*, No. 148. Caracas, Venezuela, 1973, 21-61.
Husek, T.R. and T. Sirotnik. Item Sampling in Educational Research. *Occasional Report*, February 1967, No. 2.
Kerlinger, F.N. *Foundations of Behavioral Research*. New York: Holt, Rinehart and Winston, 1967.
Miller, O.M. y R.W. Wolfe. Que apreden en la escuela los estudiantes. *Planeamientos y Metodologicos*, Serie 3, No. 4. Departamento de Investigaciones Educacionales, Direccion de Planeamiento, Ministerio de Educacion, Caracas, Venezuela, 1973, 75-98.
Thorndike, R.L. and E.P. Hagen. *Measurement and Evaluation in Psychology and Education*. New York: John Wiley and Sons, 1969.

# Teacher Evaluation and Domain-Referenced Measurement

W. James Popham

Perhaps it is only overdue retribution that so many American teachers are now trying to dodge buckshot from the same scatter-guns that they have leveled at their pupils for so many years. And the frightening feature of facing a scatter-gun is that it is hard to tell where the pellets are coming from. Most tests that teachers have fired at their pupils through the decades have behaved in a similar manner, that is, the learners were hard put to anticipate the nature of the expectations being tossed at them. But now, as a consequence of an increasingly accountability-conscious citizenry, we find teachers being obliged to demonstrate their own proficiency on the same ill-defined measurement devices that have historically perplexed their students.

## Snowballing Teacher Appraisal

It is interesting to conjecture regarding the reasons for the public's current disenchantment with our school system. Maybe it is dismay over the perennially low performance of so many children on standardized reading achievement tests (without a recognition by the public that *by their nature* such tests must classify half of all children as reading below grade level). Possibly it is just a tight economy, in which a person with fewer dollars in his pocket is more prudent about how he

W. James Popham is at the University of California, Los Angeles.

spends them—increased school taxes representing a perceived luxury. But whatever the causes, American taxpayers are now determined to get their money's worth out of public education. And one of the ways they intend to do so is by evaluating school teachers.

## Teacher Evaluation Programs

In an increasing number of school districts across the nation, we find that boards of education have required school administrators to initiate more systematic systems of appraising district teaching personnel. At the state level, the most notable instance of an increased demand for teacher appraisal is in California, where the law now requires all teachers in the state to be evaluated in terms of their ability to produce demonstrable results with children. The California law, generally referred to as the Stull Act* after its author, Assemblyman John Stull, has produced an enormous amount of activity in that state, as local school districts have attempted to design the teacher appraisal system established by the 1971 state legislature. Although there is considerable latitude open to local districts regarding the particulars of their teacher appraisal systems, there are no options with respect to the necessity to secure indications of learner progress in each area of study.

Thus, in California, because of state mandate, and in other locales because of dissatisfaction with the customary process criteria (e.g., classroom observations and administrator ratings), teacher evaluation systems are being devised which pay particular attention to the appraisal of instruction in terms of its impact on pupils. Not surprisingly, therefore, we find such systems relying heavily on test results secured from learners. While theoretically we are at liberty to measure a wide range of learner behaviors, not just test results, in our efforts to gauge the influence of a teacher's efforts, a variety of factors currently incline us to lean heavily on paper-and-pencil measures. And it is through the use of typical testing procedures that a host of America's teachers will find their feathers somewhat singed, if not outright burned off.

## Typical Tests and Their Terrors

Both for the learners obliged to complete them and the teachers

---

*For a further discussion of the Stull Act, see W. James Popham. California's Precedent-Setting New Teacher Evaluation Law. *Educational Researcher,* July 1972, *1*, 7.

who will be judged on the basis of that learner performance, customary testing procedures have little to commend them. For example, the most common testing tactic involves the use of commercially distributed standardized tests. These tests, often referred to as *norm-referenced* measures because they are designed to measure an individual's performance in relationship to the performance of a normative group, suffer from two major deficiencies as far as teacher evaluation is concerned.

First, because norm-referenced tests must produce considerable score variance among those completing the test, there is a danger that test items will be excluded which might prove useful in detecting the results of instruction. For example, items which are answered correctly by most learners after instruction would have to be modified or eliminated from the test since such items would not contribute sufficiently to individuals' variance. In time, particularly with standardized tests which have been revised often, these instruments become less and less sensitive to picking up those kinds of pupil growth which teachers often strive to produce. For if a large proportion of teachers are becoming successful in promoting a given type of learner behavior, the test items which detect this increasingly homogeneous high performance will be discarded because they fail to produce their share of discrimination. Now, for the purpose for which most norm-referenced tests were designed, that is, to spread people out, test items which discriminate among people are fine. But for teacher evaluation based on learner performance, a standardized achievement test which contains many such items does not give the teacher an even break.

A second and, for purposes of this analysis, an even more distressing shortcoming of most standardized tests is that they are woefully imprecise in detailing the kinds of learner behaviors being assessed. Many standardized tests in reading, for example, merely yield global scores on "comprehension" or "decoding skills." Yet, each of these rubrics covers a host of specific skills we may be trying to promote for particular learners. The teacher who is to be evaluated on the basis of learner performance on such measures will be hard put to figure out exactly what the sought-for learner behaviors really are. As any person can tell you who has been evaluated adversely without knowing what the evaluative criteria are, it is pretty scary business.

While not all teacher evaluation schemes rely on standardized tests, many others employ locally devised tests which, apart from the site of their birth, for all practical purposes were developed like standardized tests and thus behave like standardized tests.

## Domain-Referenced Tests as an Alternative

An alternative testing strategy which corrects most of the deficits of standardized tests and their locally produced counterparts requires the use of domain-referenced tests. While the critical elements of domain-referenced measures have been detailed earlier in this book, it should be noted that the domain of learner behavior under scrutiny need not consist exclusively of the more common cognitive achievement behaviors, but can tap affectively oriented learner behaviors as well. The really critical attribute of a domain-referenced measure is that it is based on a detailed description of the nature of learner behaviors to be assessed.

Because of its great effort to clarify the behavior domain being measured, a domain-referenced test offers teachers a far better idea of what the test really assesses and, therefore, what to promote in the learner. This increased clarity of intent is invaluable to an instructor, not only in initially designing an instructional sequence but, perhaps more importantly, in deciding on corrective action if the instruction proves unsuccessful. (Baker, this book, discusses in detail how DRT helps to clarify the teacher's tasks.)

In California, for instance, the new teacher evaluation law calls for districts to offer improvement programs to teachers who have received negative evaluations. If such improvement efforts cannot be focused on the types of learner behaviors to be sought, they will more likely than not consist of such feckless admonitions as "Go, thou, and teach—better!"

A set of precise delineations of the category of learner behaviors to be measured by a test can offer the astute teacher a pile of guidelines regarding how to develop an instructional sequence which will promote learner mastery of the domain. Too much instruction now fails because of a lack of clear understanding on the part of the teacher regarding what the nature of the desired terminal behavior really is.

Another advantage of domain-referenced tests is that they will be more sensitive to the results of instruction than their norm-referenced counterparts. This increased sensitivity stems largely from their freedom of the requirement to produce a high degree of between-student score variance. If most learners can, at the close of instruction, master a given behavior domain as reflected by their performance on a domain-referenced test—all the better. We need not discard such tests if they really assess important kinds of learner behaviors.

### Difficulties of Domain-Delineation

But while domain-referenced tests offer considerable promise for outcome-focused teacher evaluation, we should not underestimate the difficulties associated with carving out the requisite domain descriptions. It is devilishly difficult work. For this reason the architects of teacher evaluation systems should either devote considerable resources to the domain delineation phase of the system's development or make use of some of the domain-referenced measures which are beginning to be available from various agencies. (Considerable resources must be devoted to domain delineation in any case, since commercially available domain-referenced testing systems vary widely in quality and coverage and they must be carefully evaluated by the user to insure that they serve his purposes.)

### Sharpening the Teacher's Skills

To the extent that teachers are being forced to display their competence in promoting learner mastery of well-defined domains of learner behaviors, it seems a professional if not a moral responsibility of educational leaders to offer them support at becoming more skilled in this endeavor. Some promising developments have occurred recently in the provision of instructor improvement materials through which a teacher can develop increased skills in the ability to promote student mastery of prespecified instructional objectives.

If staff development programs can be devised which increase the teacher's expertise in aiding learners to master explicit instructional objectives, and this increased skill can be used to facilitate the learner's attainment on domain-referenced tests, then perhaps the anxieties associated with widespread teacher evaluation can be allayed. There is nothing like competence plus clarified criteria to reduce a teacher's tensions.

# Planning for Evaluation in Performance Contracting Experiments: The Connection to Domain-Referenced Testing Theory

Guilbert C. Hentschke and
Donald M. Levine

Our general purpose in this chapter is to delineate the probable impact of incorporating domain-referenced testing (DRT) concepts into performance contracts (Hentschke, 1971; Levine, 1972; Rand Corporation, 1971; Stucker and Hall, 1971). The task is not a trivial one, because from the viewpoints of both research and practice, the most important issue in performance contracting for education may well be that of measurement, testing and evaluation, and the consequent planning and policy implications.

In performance contracting, obviously we must evaluate performance in order to determine contractor payments. The utility of evaluation for this purpose depends at least as much on the payment schedule (which links performance measurement to payment) as it does on the actual measures and tests used, for the schedule may be adjusted to offset suspected inequalities and errors in the tools of measurement. Still, the validity of such tools is a basic problem that has resulted in a variety of criticisms. Opinions differ as to what are the major testing issues in performance contracting. However, the issues usually deal with

Guilbert C. Hentschke and Donald M. Levine are at Teachers College, Columbia University.

one or more of the problem areas outlined below. These problem areas are not all mutually exclusive, but each individually seems to warrant attention. Each of these problem areas is briefly sketched, and is followed by a brief discussion about how (if at all) domain-referenced testing may help to deal with the difficulty.

### Problem I: Tests don't match the goals of the program.

A frequent criticism of performance-contracting testing programs relates to the general inappropriateness of tests and test items. Specialized programs require specialized testing instruments. It is obviously more difficult to develop specialized testing instruments than it is to buy a ready-made, standardized instrument whose items are *generally* "close" to the objectives of the program.

Part of the problem lies in the pervasive lack of clearly stated goal and objective hierarchies from which appropriate test items can be developed. The "fit" between current program objectives and testing instruments is still relatively loose. (See Bruno, 1972; and Carpenter and Hall, 1971.)

### Enter Domain-Referenced Testing (DRT) Theory.

DRT Theory may hold some promise for tying assessment instruments more closely to the stated goals and objectives of performance contracting programs. Clearly, separating teaching responsibilities from testing responsibilities is a necessary but not sufficient measure. In fact, it is an increased awareness and dialogue between teachers and testers which DRT theorists advocate as a method of improving the fit between program objectives and testing and instruments. (See chapters by Baker, Popham and Miller.)

### Problem II: Individual test instruments are inadequate in assessing all program objectives.

This criticism differs from the one above in that even "very close" tests measure only a fraction of the kinds of outcomes in a performance contracting situation. A test which adequately assesses how well a student reads rarely will also assess how well he likes reading (assuming both are general objectives of the program). Because performance contracting compensation plans are tied closely to testing results, use of multiple testing instruments might compound the complexity of an already highly subjective process.

Enter DRT Theory.

It does not seem that if DRT were used in current performance contracting situations, it would go very far in helping to alleviate this structural problem. For purely pragmatic reasons, payoff schedules are tied to one or two skill testing instruments. But, theoretically, it is possible to link multiple instruments (say a reading test and an attitude survey) to a payoff schedule. Indeed, some performance contracting payoff schedules are constructed as a function of two scores. For example, in the performance contract between the Dallas Independent School District and New Century, the pay schedule was a function of (1) standardized achievement test gains in years and (2) average percent of items answered correctly on five interim performance tests. This notion would be expanded to more test instruments (either domain-referenced or norm-referenced) testing different kinds of skills and attitudes.

**Problem III: Some program goals are inherently more difficult to measure than others.**

Performance contracts have focused primarily on reading and mathematics programs. Although it is true that these basic skills are critical to the over-all school program, it is no coincidence that testing instruments are much better developed in these areas than in most other "academic" subjects. Part of this problem stems from not developing relatively concise objectives in, for example, social studies projects. (This applies not only to the "subject matter" objectives, but also to the affective objectives discussed earlier.) Because compensation strategies are based upon performance measures, this problem is fundamental to broader applications of performance contracting for instruction.

Enter DRT Theory.

This problem appears to be fundamental to testing in general. Determining behavioral profiles for learning generates problems for both the norm-referenced test constructor and the domain-referenced test constructor.

**Problem IV: Evaluation designs cannot at this time separate out the contribution to learning resulting from an instructional program from contributions from extra-program factors.**

Most program evaluation efforts are based on the assumption that any program gains (or lack thereof) that are found at the end of a period of instruction (for example, a school year) are due entirely to that program. This assumption persists despite the acknowledged influence of non-program and non-school factors on achievement. It is commonplace to talk about the impact of "home," "peer group," etc. on school achievement and the lack of uniform impact of school variables on achievement (Averch et al., 1974; Coleman, 1966; Hanushek, 1970; Jencks, 1972; Michelson, 1970). Yet the marginal impact of, for example, different types of home environments on achievement in reading by grade three is only vaguely conceived. And certainly this type of analysis is not incorporated in current performance contracting testing efforts.

**Enter DRT Theory.**

This, of course, is part of the larger problem of trying to determine what difference schools make in learning. It has to do with the relationship of causes to effects, and it remains a problem no matter what measures are chosen to show the effects. So DRT theory does not necessarily help.

**Problem V: Determining appropriate levels of achievement for a program and linking them to payoff schedules is, at best, a highly intuitive process in performance contracting.**

In part because we cannot factor out the unique contribution of a program, we have difficulty in determining how well a particular child *should* be performing in a given instructional program (Morris, 1967). For a number of reasons, relying on data which tell how some sample of students in the same grade performed is subject to much criticism (Coleman and Karweit, 1972).

This problem is fundamental to performance contracting because *a priori* levels of expectation are linked to payoff schedules. Without a well-defined method for deriving reasonably valid performance expectancies, neither the contractor nor the educational organization is sure what the chances are that they are "getting taken." Evidence to date shows that neither side is accruing significant savings or profits (Carpenter and Hall, 1971). This is due in part to the development of relatively low-risk/low-gain payoff/penalty schedules, which again reflects little knowledge about probable outcomes.

# Performance Contracting Experiments

**Enter DRT Theory.**
It is in dealing with this problem that domain-referenced testing theory can make a substantial improvement in the quality of performance contracting systems. The theory behind developing response probabilities can be fruitfully extended to analyses of probable payoff for given payoff schedules. By gradually establishing requisite data on probable responses of very specific student populations to specific items, "the art" of constructing performance payoff schedules may be improved.

**Problem VI: Using gain scores in interpreting program effect is technically too unreliable.**
The individual achievement test gain scores often used to compute payments do not reflect actual achievement only. As Stake and Wardrop (1971) have put it, gain scores may "assure the appearance of learning where there is no learning at all" because "the conventional achievement test does not have the necessary content validity for individual student achievement." The large proportion of error and low reliability of simple individual gain computed by taking the arithmetic difference of pre- and posttest scores make gain scores a dangerous basis for payments. Some of this danger can be allayed by penalizing the contractor for achievement losses to the same extent he is rewarded for gains, which will average out fortuitous over- and under-payments; by focusing on group gain scores, which should average out errors before payment is made; or by mathematically dropping out a percentage of error to derive "actual" achievement scores. But each of these solutions has its own, mainly operational drawbacks.

**Enter DRT Theory.**
The main advantage of having a cleanly defined test domain is that one can sample repeatedly from it. This would make it possible to base a payoff schedule not simply on pre-post gains, but on the slope of a growth curve described by monthly, weekly or even daily tests. (See Ann Dell Duncan's chapter.) The problem of determining appropriate payoff slopes is essentially equivalent to the problem of determining appropriate payoff levels.

**Problem VII: It is difficult to factor out learning which is "lasting" vs. learning which is superficial or short-range.**
This problem is significant in letting performance contracts if two

assumptions are made: (1) different instructional strategies can influence changes in rate of retention; and (2) current performance contracting systems happen to be structured in such a way that short-term learning effects (nine months or less) are rewarded at the expense of longer term effects. Standardized tests are least helpful here (Stake, 1971).

### Enter DRT Theory.

This problem appears to be tied more to the general structure of current performance contracting systems than to the particular mode of test construction. Changes required here would probably be in the area of time of tests and payoffs rather than mode of testing. That is, part of the compensation for a particular contract could be tied to, say, a *"post hoc* plus one semester" test.

### Problem VIII: Rigidly designed criteria encourage teaching to the test.

Within certain educational/training programs "teaching to the test" is an entirely defensible instructional strategy. A reasonable objective of a typing course, for example, might be "to have each student typing at 40 words per minute with less than 15 percent error after 20 hours of instruction." Such an objective needs no major redefinition or clarification to serve the purposes of performance contracting. It is sufficiently specific for both parties to know that task must be performed. Also it is easy to derive unequivocal performance measures from this objective, thus eliminating the possibility of serious testing—and hence remunerative—distortion.

Yet even this seemingly clear-cut example can serve to point up possible abuses of teaching to the test. If at test time students were confronted with a particular manuscript with which they were very familiar, their type of performance could be markedly superior to the case in which students were typing from an unfamiliar manuscript.

### Enter DRT Theory.

The dilemma between (1) validly testing program objectives and (2) testing just the *specific examples* used during instruction is just that—a dilemma. The two concepts tend to be directly related to each other; when we try to maximize the former we tend to minimize the latter. But DRT offers the opportunity to agree precisely on a middle ground. By defining a large set of potential test manuscripts, formed, for example, by collecting all the letters written during a given period of time by the secretarial pool for a large business, and informing teachers and students that they will be tested on samples from that set, the dangers of teaching for a specific test may be minimized.

**Problem IX: Extreme emphasis on mastering specific objectives could have negative affective spinoffs.**

Related to the previous problem is that of suboptimization: more explicitly stated objectives are maximized at the expense of less explicitly stated objectives. Those portions of a school's total curriculum that seem least appropriate for a performance contract are those with high normative or affective content. It is hard to pinpoint these portions of curriculum since training programs and basic skills programs themselves have significant noncognitive aspects; but we might look to the curriculum as a whole to have more affective influence than any of its parts. Clearly, the total curriculum of a program and its more affective portion share the same problem in performance contracting, i.e., highly debatable outputs that generally defy meaningful quantification. It is important to realize that the affective results of a performance contract for any portion of a curriculum are questionable, and few efforts have been made to define or limit those results.

Given the contractor's profit maximizing behavior, which usually is channeled only by certain cognitive objectives and measures and constrained only by time and resource specifications, a performance contracting program may well have serious, unforeseen affective consequences (Levine, 1972, p. 10). Moreover, such change can be unpredictable, and, from the school administrator's point of view, uncontrollable. Two of the recent performance contracts that involve an entire curriculum (Gary, Indiana and Jacksonville, Florida) seem to have recognized this difficulty, for they tie payment only to the reading and math parts of their program (Levine, 1972).

**Enter DRT Theory.**

Does DRT Theory offer a unique way to get at this particular problem? We think not. This problem appears to be a general one of measuring "learning," and not one of a particular referent (norm or criteria).

Problem X: There is virtually no theoretical guideline that can be used to determine the appropriate mix of resources used for instruction and resources used for evaluation.

A fundamental concern within the context of performance contracting has to do with determining the ratio of (1) resources to be devoted to program evaluation to (2) resources to be devoted to program operation. Usually the two figures are inversely related to each other; that is, at a given budget level, resources which are deployed to program evaluation are resources which could have been deployed to "improve" or "beef up" program operation. The "appropriate" mix of operation and evaluation resources depends in large part on the use(s) to which evaluation data in a performance contracting setting form a basis for contractor compensation (over and above needs for general program assessment); proportionately more resources must be devoted to evaluation. Even so, one approaches a point of diminishing returns when the additional dollar spent on program evaluation to yield more "accurate" data would be better spent on program operation to generate greater program impact.

**Enter DRT Theory.**

The same problem would persist whether or not domain-referenced testing practices were implemented in evaluation of performance contracted programs. In fact, it is possible that proportionately more resources might have to be devoted to program evaluation (at the expense of short-term program impact). In tailoring his evaluation instruments to each different program the domain-referenced tester would have to develop (1) a network of item forms (which specifies the domain of items); (2) an assignment plan (which specifies the testing system that refers to the domain); (3) an administration procedure (which specifies the experimental conditions under which the data are gathered); and (4) response probabilities (empirically derived documentation of expected responses). (See chapters by Hively and Millman, this book.)

As outlined in greater detail by others, domain-referenced testing theory represents a qualitatively "better" but relatively more expensive evaluation tool in a performance contracting context. It is an open question whether the increase in the quality of the evaluation more than justifies the resulting opportunity cost.

**Problem XI:** Too much emphasis is placed on discrimination among students and not enough attention is given to assessing the degree of accomplishment of goals of the program.

The explanation for such a state in educational program evaluation is traceable to the use of norm-referenced, standardized tests. Schools largely measure student achievement relative to other students, and their results are expressed in relative terms. The use of relative measures means that as performance levels change in the norming population, either the norms must be changed (which would preclude over-time comparisons) or the relative measures will no longer accurately express the child's or the school's standing relative to the current population (Coleman and Karweit, 1972). (Even if performance levels do not change, the fact that norms are always based on a given grade level makes it difficult to measure relative growth by comparing performance at different levels.)

The problems inherent in interpreting norm-referenced testing data are significant. The fundamental rationale for using norms should, however, be kept in mind. Norms provide a means for comparing groups of students included in a performance contract program with "comparable" students who are not in the program. The notion of comparing student achievement results with those of referent or "control" group is both useful and intuitively appealing. A very frequent criticism of standardized testing in a performance contracting situation is about the "appropriateness" of a *particular* norming group, not about systematic reference to *a* norming group.

**Enter DRT Theory.**

Domain-referenced testing would differ theoretically from current practice in at least one significant way: standards used to select test items. For domain-referenced tests, each item would be written so that a correct answer indicates attainment of some important element of achievement in the subject matter of the test. That the item may be answered correctly by most examinees, and, hence discriminate poorly (by the usual measures of item discrimination) is of little concern. With domain-referenced testing, the relevance of the item to the goals of achievement is more important than the information it provides on differences in achievement among students. Given two items of nearly equal relevance to the goals of instruction, the norm-referenced test constructor will choose the one that discriminates better between students of high and low achievement.

It is important for a number of reasons to assess performance against a standard. When payment schedules are to be tied to testing results, contract letters by definition are basing compensation plans on *some* standards. Standardized test instruments provide a standard of past performance by a norming group. Domain-referenced test instruments generate standards through an empirically derived "response probability," i.e., the chances that, when a given stimulus is presented, a given response will occur, within a given interval of time.

One estimates probabilities by observing frequencies: by presenting members of the "same" class of stimuli repeatedly to members of the "same" class of subjects, under the "same" class of conditions, and observing whether or not members of the "same" class of responses occur. In other words, a probability is estimated by taking a sample of observations from a set of possible observations. *The general experimental problem is to define the set of possible observations precisely enough, and to sample systematically enough, that the estimates derived from the samples show orderly relationships to independent variables of interest* (Hively, 1972, emphasis added).

Such a *theory* is clearly superior to the *current state* of norm-referenced testing *practices*. Not unlike the discrepancy between theory and practice in norm-referenced testing, however, the chasm between theory and practice in domain-referenced testing could be equally difficult to bridge. Within the context of performance contracting systems it is the latest testing *practices* (not the latest testing *theory*) which must guide the educator's actions. It is hard to see how the practical problems inherent in domain-referenced testing (e.g., determining the "same" class of test conditions) are any less difficult to overcome than those inherent in norm-referenced testing (e.g., assessing the "appropriate" norming groups).

**Conclusion**

Having reviewed briefly some of the current testing problems in performance contracting, what then can we say about the potential of domain-referenced testing for helping to alleviate them?

1. There appear to be several testing problems in performance

## Performance Contracting Experiments

contracting that are common to all types of testing including domain-referenced testing and norm-referenced testing. For example, in the case of developing behavioral proxies of attitudes, a generally defensible measure of "love of mathematics" is as difficult to develop for a domain-referenced test as for a norm-referenced test.

2. A large part of the testing problems encountered in performance contracting are traceable, not to the theory of norm-referenced testing, but to the discrepancy between theory and practice. For example, on the question of norming, most criticism is not directed at the concept of norming against "comparable" populations. Rather, it is directed at the operational issue of whether the norming populations in a particular case are, in fact, "comparable." It is not unreasonable to assume that a similar discrepancy would manifest itself if domain-referenced testing theory were put into practice in performance contracting.

3. Finally, even granting the above two arguments, it would appear that using domain-referenced theory in performance contracting could help to alleviate some of the current testing problems in performance contracting. These problem areas would include, but not be limited to (a) matching test items to program objectives; (b) developing *theoretically* defensible matrices of expected performances, thereby reducing the relatively arbitrary construction of payoff schedules; (c) placing more emphasis on accomplishment of program objectives and less on discrimination among students; and, possibly, (d) providing a workable alternative to gain scores as a means of measuring program effect.

Within the over-all context of testing problem areas in performance contracting, the above four are not insignificant. The increased cost which seems inherent in using domain-referenced testing may be more than justified. At the very least, the question should be raised and analyzed on an experimental basis. The utility of domain-referenced testing for more effective planning (and hence evaluation) of performance contracting in education can be properly assessed only after a longer period of basic DRT and evaluation research and collection of more significant data on actual use in performance contracting programs. Its potential as a device for more realistic evaluation in planning for performance contracting requires further exploration.

## References

Averch, H.A. *et al. How Effective Is Schooling? A Critical Review of Research.* Englewood Cliffs, N.J.: Educational Technology Publications, 1974.
Bruno, J.E. A Methodology for the Evaluation of Instruction of Performance Contracts Which Incorporates School District Utilities and Goals. *Am. Ed. Res. J.,* Spring 1972, *9,* 2, 175-195.
Carpenter, P. and G.R. Hall. *Case Studies in Educational Performance Contracting: Conclusions and Implications.* The Rand Corporation, R-900/1-HEW, December 1971.
Coleman, J.S. *et al. Equality of Educational Opportunity.* Washington, D.C.: U.S. Government Printing Office, 1966.
Coleman, J.S. and N.L. Karweit. *Information Systems and Performance Measures in Schools.* Englewood Cliffs, New Jersey: Educational Technology Publications, 1972.
Hanushek, E. *The Value of Teachers in Teaching.* Santa Monica: The Rand Corporation, December 1970.
Hentschke, G.C. (Ed.) *Performance Contracting.* Denver, Colorado: The Rocky Mountain Regional Interstate Project, E.S.E.A. V, 505, March 1971.
Hively, W. Domain-Referenced Testing. Working paper, MinneMast Project, University of Minnesota, fall 1972 (mimeo).
Jencks, C. *et al. Inequality: A Reassessment of the Effect of Family and Schooling in America.* New York: Basic Books, Inc., 1972.
Levine, D.M. *The National Conference on Performance Contracting: Final Report.* Washington, D.C.: U.S. Department of Health, Education and Welfare, Project No. 1-0616, June 1972.
Michelson, S. The Association of Teacher Resourcefulness with Children's Characteristics. In *Do Teachers Make a Difference?* Washington, D.C.: U.S. Government Printing Office, September 1970.
Morris, L.R. Cost-Effectiveness: The Current State of the Art. Unpublished doctoral dissertation, Harvard University, 1967.
The Rand Corporation. *Case Studies in Educational Performance Contracting,* R-900/1-HEW through R-900/6-HEW. Santa Monica, 1971.
Stake, R.E. Testing Hazards in Performance Contracting. *Phi Delta Kappan,* June 1971, 583-589.
Stake, R.E. and J.L. Wardrop. Gain Score Errors in Performance Contracting, a paper presented to the American Educational Research Association, February 1971.
Stucker, J.P. and G.R. Hall. *The Performance Contracting Concept in Education.* Santa Monica: The Rand Corporation, R-692/1-HEW, May 1971.

# Program and Product Evaluation from a Domain-Referenced Viewpoint

Thomas J. Johnson

Contemporary educational literature reflects a growing awareness of the importance of domain-referenced testing as a framework for the evaluation of products and programs. Many attempts to utilize this framework have, however, run into serious difficulties. This has been due in part to lack of a standard terminology and a thorough conceptualization of the basic theory and, in larger measure, to lack of a carefully explicated set of item generative procedures, statistical models and analytic routines governing implementation. The purpose of this chapter is to focus attention on some of the more important factors to be considered in evaluating educational products and programs within the domain-referenced framework.

According to Mesthene (1970), Harvard specialist in technology transfer, the term "technology" refers to the organization of knowledge for the achievement of practical purposes. Examples of technology, according to his definition, include not only machines but also intellectual tools, analytic and mathematic techniques and other types of "products" usually associated with the output of social science. Among these we may include educational products, programs and intervention procedures. Another authority, Strasser (1970), states that the evaluation of technology is a "systematic planning and forecasting

Thomas J. Johnson is with CEMREL, Inc., St. Louis, Missouri.

process that delineates options and costs, encompassing economic as well as environmental and social considerations, that are both external and internal to the program or project in question with special focus on technology-related 'bad' as well as 'good' effects." In this sense, educational product and program evaluation can be considered a special case of technology evaluation.

From the technological viewpoint, an educational program may be thought of as a system of components intended to produce a specific set of outcomes. Each component consists of a theoretically important activity or function to be generated by some educational product, e.g., a book, toy, teacher's guide or unit. (It does not matter whether the products are experimentally developed or spontaneously constructed, commercially produced or teacher made.) To evaluate such a program, one must have a description of (a) theoretically important activities or functions which make up each component, (b) the outcomes each activity is intended to produce, (c) the ways the outcomes are to be measured and (d) the rationale connecting $a$, $b$ and $c$. To address this complex set of causal relationships, I believe that the evaluator needs more complex mathematical models, sampling designs and statistical analyses than are now in use. Moreover, I believe that the assessment of these causal relationships requires a domain-referenced framework of analysis.

## The Analysis of Educational Products and Programs

Formal knowledge in any given area may be thought of as consisting of the following information: (1) descriptions of the phenomena of interest: objects, persons, events, etc.; (2) descriptions of the methods and devices used to observe or regulate the phenomena; and (3) descriptions of important properties and relationships manifested by the phenomena (Johnson, 1972). The knowledge generated by an educational product may be usefully described under these headings.

With this as a starting point, an idealized flow of educational product development, from basic research stages to the final form as it is utilized in instruction, can be conceptualized. An educational product is a set of causal elements intended to reliably produce a certain subset of properties of a class of phenomena, in such a way that someone can learn about them. The form of the product is influenced

*Program and Product Evaluation* 99

by such desirable features as low cost, ease of manufacture, durability, etc., and this has powerful implications for both instruction and evaluation, because the form of the product provides the basis for relating the property set taken to be the content of instruction to the properties of the test-item domain utilized for evaluation.

By way of illustration, consider the *Frisbee*, the plastic disk that can be sailed back and forth from person to person. This product represents aerodynamic properties of convex and concave circular objects launched with a rotating motion. The manufactured "toy" captures the properties required for long-range sailing. A domain of types of Frisbee throws (similar to that of "wing shots" described by Hively in Part One of this book) can be readily defined to represent the skills associated with the phenomenon. And a domain of tasks involving transformation of the structure of the disk can be defined to represent the understanding of its basic aerodynamic properties. Similarly, any educational game or activity exemplifies certain property sets of a phenomenon of interest.

The focus of attention in this discussion will be on the evaluation of the hard products (machines, games, devices, toys) and the pedagogical products (textbooks, curriculum materials, lessons) which form the basis for most educational activities in elementary, secondary and college classrooms, and which are often integrated to form a "program" of instruction.

To get a feeling for the complexity of the practical problems involved in evaluating components of a large instructional program, consider this application. A school district has set up a screening procedure for children who plan to enroll in kindergarten in the fall for the purpose of providing an instructional program to help those preschool children who are found to have certain skill deficiencies related to the kindergarten objectives. This instructional program will be implemented by the parents of the preschool children, through the use of instructional packages (games, lessons, etc.) which are related to each of the skill areas. The teachers in the district will develop these packages for use by the parents.

While such a program might reasonably be undertaken by any good school system, it provides a formidable problem for the program or product evaluator. The following discussion will present a conceptualization of the domains relevant to this kind of program which would permit a reasonable evaluation of the total program, and the differentiated "products" embedded in it.

## The Characterization of Domains

There are five distinct classes of elements which supply the raw material for any domain-referenced evaluation effort. These classes are as follows:
1. A domain of educational goals, i.e., a set of objectives.
2. A domain of information, i.e., a set of knowledge elements.
3. A domain of technology, i.e., a set of educational products.
4. A domain of instruction, i.e., a set of educational activities.
5. A domain of performance, i.e., a set of test items.

To relate the elements of these five domains, it is absolutely necessary to assimilate them into a common conceptual scheme.

The *domain of educational objectives* provides the rationale for selecting elements for the other four domains. Objectives are defined in many ways: (1) as a set of valued experiences, perceptual, affective or cognitive; (2) as a set of purposive skills to be attained, e.g., (a) methods of controlling the phenomena of interest, (b) methods of observing these phenomena, or (c) methods of analyzing and describing the phenomena; (3) as a set of modes of perception to be utilized or developed, e.g., kinesthetic, visual, auditory, tactile, olfactory.

The *domain of information* is the knowledge base related to each of the various objectives of the program. It requires (1) specification of the phenomena of interest; (2) the properties, attributes, attribute-values and relations to be observed and studied; (3) the method of observation, presentation or regulation of these properties; and (4) the language used to describe the properties.

The *domain of technology* is the set of products used in the program, described in terms of (1) the aspects of the phenomena of interest, captured or embedded in each product, and (2) the specific language of instruction utilized in, or related to, the product.

The *domain of instruction* is what the teacher actually does. It requires explication of (1) how each of the phenomena of interest is represented in the products as they are used in the classroom, and (2) the language system(s) for dealing with these phenomena across the products used.

The *domain of performance* represents the enormous (and mainly hypothetical) set of items that might be generated to reflect all of the "knowledge" about a given field of interest related to a given set of objectives. While the task of specifying all of these items is impractical, nevertheless the parameters of the item universe can and *must* be defined. This will provide the basis for later generation of items. The evaluator needs to specify (1) the behavioral outcomes desired with respect to the phenomena included in the domain of content and the goals included in the domain of objectives, and (2) the language system for the outcomes (corresponding to the language system of the products used in instruction). Following a procedure like that described by Baker, the evaluator must also specify (3) the response methodologies to be used in detecting the outcomes;* (4) the set of item formats or grammatical forms to be used; and (5) the set of appropriate occasions, situations or contexts for the occurrence of behavioral outcomes. These aspects of the domain of items are more formally differentiated in this paper than in previous discussions of domain-referenced testing, and I hope the value of this differentiation will become apparent as the discussion continues, and as the concept of domain weighting is introduced.

## Causal Inference in
## Domain-Referenced Testing

In the preceding section the idea of domain-referenced evaluation has been expanded to include domains of objectives, knowledges, products and instructional content, as well as items. The importance of each of these, and the information function they serve, can best be represented by the following chart.

| Domain | Information Function |
|---|---|
| 1. Objective | 1. What we want to do |
| 2. Knowledge | 2. What we know |
| 3. Products | 3. What we can possibly do, demonstrate or effectuate with the available means. |
| 4. Instruction | 4. What we actually do with the available means |
| 5. Items | 5. What we measure with |

*Response methodologies commonly used in testing include: matching, recognition, identification, written production, oral production, manual production, written reproduction, oral reproduction, manual reproduction, categorization, ranking, pair of N-item comparisons, ratings and estimation.

Ideally there should be reasonable correspondence between at least two pairs of these domains for strong inferences to be drawn from any evaluation effort. For example, there must be close correspondence between the domain of objectives and the domain of instruction (what we want to do and what we actually do); and equally close correspondence between the domain of instruction and the domain of test items (what we actually do and what we measure with).

The degree of correspondence between the domain of objectives and the instruction domain is mediated less directly by the knowledge base, i.e., what we know, and more directly by the domain of products which have been derived from the knowledge base, as these products represent the means of translating the knowledge to the student group. Noncorrespondence of these two domains can occur for a number of reasons, e.g., lack of knowledge, lack of products, product failure, nonuse or misuse of products, poor product description, and the like, but is most often due to inadequate content evaluation during development.

The appropriate causal model for evaluating a program, or a constituent product, may be constructed by specifying which element or cluster of elements of each domain is to be mapped onto or into the elements or clusters of elements of another. If any elements of any domain are not mappable, (1) they can be dropped from the model, (2) one or more of the domains can be further differentiated to effect the desired mapping or (3) several domain elements can be collapsed for the same result. When the mappability of elements is distributed across subjects, or across groups within treatments, or across product sets within programs, then a weighting system may be applied to the mapping function based on the proportionality of this correspondence. This permits causal models at several levels of precision to be evaluated.

A "program" versus "no program" evaluation would be one in which few of the elements in the above domains were differentiated very well. If the effects attributable to a program are large ones, no major problems may be experienced using this type of model. However, such a global evaluation effort would not permit the differential analyses of program elements that might help to explain a weak program effect, or which might lead to greater program efficiency, or which might eliminate elements which are superfluous. Only a domain-referenced, causal evaluation model is capable of these discriminations. But partially differentiated or "fully" differentiated causal

*Program and Product Evaluation*

models can only be applied to well-described programs. (Individual *product* evaluation would involve mapping across these same domains with the product set restricted to the one element corresponding to the product of interest.)

From the foregoing, it should now be apparent that a test constructed to evaluate the full set of outcomes of one program may not be sensitive to the outcomes of another program, so it follows that under some conditions programs may not be meaningfully compared on any common score basis. At the same time it should be clear that a test constructed to measure a program's planned objectives may not be sensitive to many of the program's actual outcomes. In this case, any single or composite score may be misleading for decision purposes. The only practical way out of such situations is to explicate all of the important elements of a program in a causal model of the evaluation effort by using the conceptualization of domains advanced earlier. It may then be possible to use a *domain weighting* procedure, derived from the relationship between treatment components and various items and subscores to arrive at a set of reasonable indices of performance for two separate treatments. The effective set of program elements in two programs, i.e., the operational components, can in this way be distinguished from the conceptual ones. Such procedures are especially critical when variation in the degree of implementation of a program across classes is likely, or where the range of curriculum materials varies across teachers, or where individualization of instruction is deliberately attempted.

Returning to the preschool program discussed earlier, the major elements that need to be explicated are depicted below.

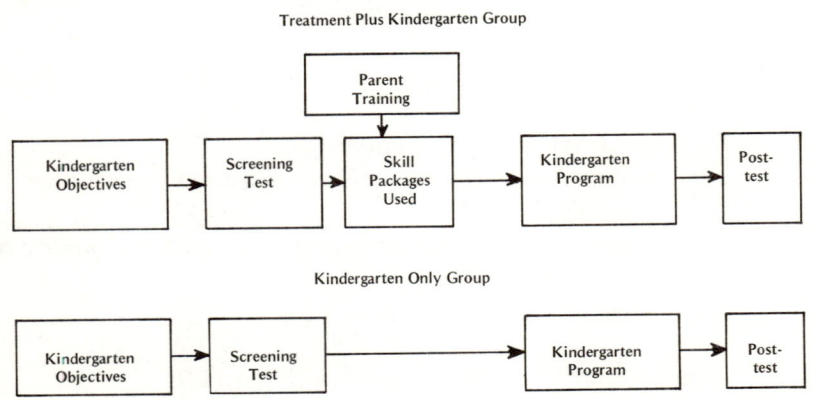

Treatment Plus Kindergarten Group

Kindergarten Objectives → Screening Test → Skill Packages Used → Kindergarten Program → Post-test

Parent Training → Skill Packages Used

Kindergarten Only Group

Kindergarten Objectives → Screening Test → Kindergarten Program → Post-test

The procedures to be followed for program characterization and subsequent evaluation are outlined below:

1. Specification of the domain of objectives for the kindergarten is required as a first step, and it is shown here to be the same for either group.

2. Following this, the items in the screening test would have to be reviewed to determine the degree to which at least the major categories of objectives are represented. Or, better still, the test might be constructed to correspond to these objectives following domain-referenced sampling procedures.

3. The items in the criterion posttest would have to be reviewed to determine the degree to which the same major categories of objectives were represented, or it would be constructed to do so as with the screening test.

4. The instructional components of the existing kindergarten program would have to be explicated, and the *a priori* correspondence of each of these components to the objectives and to each of the items of the two tests would have to be determined.

5. The elements of each package to be used by the parents would have to be explicated, and the *a priori* correspondence of each of these elements to the kindergarten objectives, the components of the kindergarten program, and each of the items of the two tests would need to be determined.

6. The actual use of packages by the parents for each student would need to be monitored to see how and to what extent each is used.

Some of the more critical comparisons and their possibly unfavorable consequences are as follows:

1. Comparison of 1 with 2 and 3; and 2 with 3.

   Possible unfavorable consequences:
   Some objectives not being measured on one or both tests.
   Some other objectives being measured by one or both tests.
   Some non-overlap between tests.

2. Comparison of 1 with 4; and 4 with 2 and 3.

# Program and Product Evaluation

Possible unfavorable consequences:
Some objectives not being attended to in kindergarten program.
Some aspects of kindergarten program outcomes not detectable in one or both tests.

3. Comparison of 1 with 5; 5 with 4; and 5 with 2 and 3.

Possible unfavorable consequences:
Some objectives not being attended to in packages.
Some packages not overlapping with kindergarten program.
Some aspects of package outcomes not detectable in posttest.

4. Comparison of 6 with 2 and 3.

Possible unfavorable consequences:
Some packages not used by the parents.

From the preceding discussion, it is clear that there are many opportunities for major weaknesses to enter into a program evaluation through lack of specification of the domains. Under *ideal* conditions the domain of objectives would be the dominant structural element in any program design. It would be the basis for generating congruent elements in the instructional program. It would provide the source of criteria for product acquisition; and it would be the basis for generating the domain of items for measuring program effects.

However, as educational program or product evaluation is presently conducted, tests get constructed and used without the benefit of a thorough causal analysis. A solution to the resulting chaos is to impose *a priori* design on the various program components; to construct a causal model of the relationships between the elements of these components and the tests used; and to weight the item set according to the structure of this model in relation to what actually went on in the program. In the case of the hypothetical preschool program: if neither the packages used by the parents nor the kindergarten program teaches skill A, the performance scores on the posttest based on items related to skill A should not be included in summary data about the efficacy of the program.

Goodness or badness of fit of a model is an important concept in program or product evaluation. The preceding discussion has focused on some of the basic problems related to the use of domain-referenced testing in evaluations. The applicability of domain-based modeling of the total program or to individual product elements and the critical importance of a common language system across all domains of interest for "causal" connecting of linked elements have been stressed as essential in determining a program's true efficacy.

### Application of Domain Weighting

That differentiated models are implementable and yield rewarding evaluation information has been evidenced by the experiences of the CEMREL staff in the evaluation of the DARCEE* preschool program in four cities. The program basically consists of some 10 sets of process variables related to the classroom and teacher, together with content related to five major domains or sets of child outcomes: basic concepts, visual skills, auditory discrimination, language development and eye-hand coordination. As the program is used in schools, there is often variation in the degree to which each process variable is implemented, and there is considerable variation at the individual child level, in the degree to which content (i.e., products) relevant to each set of child outcomes is used.

For the five sets of outcomes, content can be conceived of as a set of *major* variables, and process as a set of *minor* variables. Thus, when emphasis within a given content area varies across classes, the set of items sensitive to this given content area is likely to yield proportionally higher or lower scores, reflecting the differential emphasis. Control for these content variations within DARCEE and non-DARCEE classes was obtained by weighting the appropriate "raw" proportional score on the given domain by the degree of actual content emphasis. By way of illustration, suppose classes a, b and c varied in their emphasis on content related to item set K by proportions of .30, .60 and .90, respectively. If the proportional score over the relevant item set was .70 for each class, then class (c) would be three times less effective than class (a) in achieving outcomes related to item set K. This differential class attainment would not be detectable if the weighting procedure

---

*The Demonstration and Research Center for Early Education at George Peabody College, Nashville, Tennessee.

was not applied. In a similar manner, weighting for degree of implementation on the "process" variables can be performed. Both types of weighting may be introduced in regression analyses of the outcome data.

Further, the total test across the five DARCEE content domains could be partitioned into four different subsets of items depending on whether they utilized recognition, identification, production or reproduction types of response methodologies. Differential course emphasis related to content domains might not be so easily detected in the responses to the recognition or identification items, but might be more likely to show up in the proportions of correct responses to the production or reproduction items. Performance differences on a particular response methodology may help to pinpoint more accurately how instruction varies across classrooms. The opportunity for fine-grained analyses of this kind is available only as a consequence of strong prior design imposed on the item set, such that the elements in the appropriate domains can be related to them.

## References

Johnson, T.J. *Evaluation in the Context of Product and Program Development in Laboratory and Research and Development Centers*. Paper presented at AERA Convention, April 1972.

Mesthene, I.G. *Technological Change: Its Impact on Man and Society*. Cambridge: Harvard University Press, 1970.

Strasser, G. *Developing a Technology Assessment Capability*. Office of Science and Technology, Executive Office of the President, September 1970.

# Using Domain-Referenced Tests for Student Placement, Diagnosis and Attainment in a System of Adaptive, Individualized Instruction

Anthony J. Nitko and
Tse-Chi Hsu

"Adaptive individualized instruction" refers to an instructional system so organized and managed that the content and method vary with the individual characteristics of the learner. In its ideal form, adaptive individualized instruction uses an analysis of a student's characteristics to guide him through a course of learning especially tailored to him. To custom-tailor curriculum, we need special testing systems. Domain-referenced testing, geared to particular instructional contexts, provides a way to integrate testing and instruction so that test results can be used to guide learning rather than simply to identify the successful students.

Three Kinds of Decisions

Let us assume that an individualized course of instruction has been designed and that it has the following characteristics:
1. Terminal objectives have been specified and translated into defined domains of tasks, so that the student's performance

Anthony J. Nitko and Tse-Chi Hsu are with the Learning Research and Development Center, University of Pittsburgh.

## Student Placement, Diagnosis and Attainment

on these tasks will form the basis for inferring his attainment of the course goals.
2. A sequence of intermediate objectives leading to attainment of the terminal outcomes has been arranged.
3. Various alternative instructional procedures have been designed for each intermediate and terminal instructional goal.

Now consider how a student might most efficiently make his way through such a course. Where should he begin? What instructional procedures should he follow? How will he know when he is finished? These three questions correspond to decisions about placement, diagnosis and attainment (Glaser and Nitko, 1971).

A *placement decision* answers the question, "Where in the instructional sequence should the learner start in order to avoid repeating unnecessarily what he knows already and in order to encounter readily attainable new goals?" Tests needed to make this decision must be derived from an analysis of the psychological structure of the specific course: the processes of transfer and generalization which make it possible to order behaviors in a sequence of prerequisite tasks so that competence in an earlier task in the sequence facilitates the learning of later tasks in the sequence (Glaser and Nitko, 1971, p. 636). Tasks in this sense may be operationally defined as domains of test items, and the techniques of domain-referenced testing are readily applicable to the problem of placement.

Placement in the curriculum does not necessarily specify the methods of instruction that should be used with a particular student. Tests providing this kind of information might be called *diagnostic.* They answer the question, "What learning activities will best adapt to this student's individual requirements and thus maximize his attainment of the chosen goal?" This distinction between placement testing and diagnostic testing is not conventional. Customary diagnostic tests involve both placement and diagnosis.

The art of distinct diagnostic testing is not yet well developed. It is closely related to aptitude-treatment-interaction research (see, e.g., Cronbach and Snow, 1969; Glaser, 1972; Glaser and Nitko, 1971). From research of this kind it may be possible to develop norm-referenced aptitude tests to guide the choice of learning activities. On the other hand, diagnostic testing also involves fine-grain analysis of individual (idiosyncratic) domains of performance. What microscopic prerequisite skills are strong or weak? What misinformation or inappropriate associations may interfere with certain activities? Domain-referenced testing procedures may be adopted to answer questions such as these.

When instruction has been completed, interest centers around whether the student has learned the terminal objectives. Verbal statements of terminal objectives usually imply that an individual ought to be able to perform quite a large number of tasks. This is particularly true when generalization and transfer of learning are of primary importance. For this type of *attainment* decision, a domain-referenced testing program is essential.

## Sequences of Decisions

Before discussing how domain-referenced testing can be used to provide information for placement, diagnostic and attainment decisions in adaptive instruction, let us consider an illustration of how testing and decision-making have been integrated. The example comes from the Individually Prescribed Instruction (IPI) Project's elementary mathematics curriculum (Lindvall and Bolvin, 1967).

Figure 1 is a schematic representation of the mathematics curriculum. The content has been broken down into 10 topics which are roughly in a prerequisite order (from top to bottom in the figure). Further, each topic has been developed over a range of complex behaviors. These are also in a rough prerequisite order (from Level A through Level G in the figure). Each cell in the grid represents several instructional objectives, and is called a unit of instruction. The inset shows (hypothetically) how a short sequence of objectives might be ordered into a learning hierarchy for one unit. Each box in the hierarchy represents one objective. Usually, the hierarchy leads to a few terminal objectives (boxes "I" and "J" in the inset). Each usually draws on prerequisites from earlier topics and lower levels. (These are shown below the dotted line in the inset.)

Table 1 gives examples of some of the kinds of placement, diagnostic and attainment information that would be useful for making instructional decisions in the IPI curriculum. Figure 2 shows a flow chart of how testing and instruction blend together to guide the flow and content of instruction for each individual student. This is a hand-operated system—the "hands" being those of the pupil, teacher and teacher aide.

Figure 3 shows a flow chart of testing and teaching procedures

## Student Placement, Diagnosis and Attainment

that would be needed to implement the more elaborate system of placement, diagnostic and attainment testing previously described—a step beyond the current operating procedure illustrated in Figure 2. Although schematically more complex, this procedure can be realized relatively easily by using a computer as test administrator and information manager.

For each unit, one or more terminal objectives, and one or more subobjectives (illustrated by the boxes above the dotted line in Figure 1) are identified. Also, for each subobjective, one or more prerequisite skills found in *other* units are identified (illustrated by the boxes below the dotted line in the inset of Figure 1).

To reduce the amount of testing and to allow the student to get into instruction quickly, only terminal objectives form the basis for placement, in contrast to the system illustrated in Figure 2, which tests all objectives in the unit. Passing the tests for the terminal objectives allows the student to move on to another unit. Failing the test for one terminal objective is seen as sufficient reason to remain in the unit. The task then is to locate the pupil at the subobjective within the unit for which he needs instruction. Once the subobjective is located, the pupil is tested on relevant prerequisites from other units.

Having completed instruction for a single objective, the student's mastery is checked by a curriculum-embedded attainment test (CET). Passing the CET allows the student to cycle through the unit until all terminal objectives are mastered. If a student fails to master an objective, he is branched to an error analysis procedure—an item analysis of the test already taken plus additional testing if necessary to determine why the objective was not mastered. A remedial prescription can then be written from this information.

When all terminal objectives have been mastered as evidenced by a mastery score on the curriculum-embedded tests, the student takes an attainment test over the unit. This functions as a short term retention test in which only terminal objectives are posttested. Demonstrating mastery on the attainment test allows the student to proceed to a new unit. Mastery means " . . . that an examinee makes a sufficient number of correct responses on the sample of test tasks presented to him in order to support the generalization (from this sample of items to the domain or universe of items implied by an instruction objective) that he has attained the desired, pre-specified degree of proficiency with respect to the domain (Glaser and Nitko, 1971, p. 641)."

## Figure 1

### Example of Curriculum Layout for Individually Prescribed Instruction Elementary Mathematics

Level of Complexity

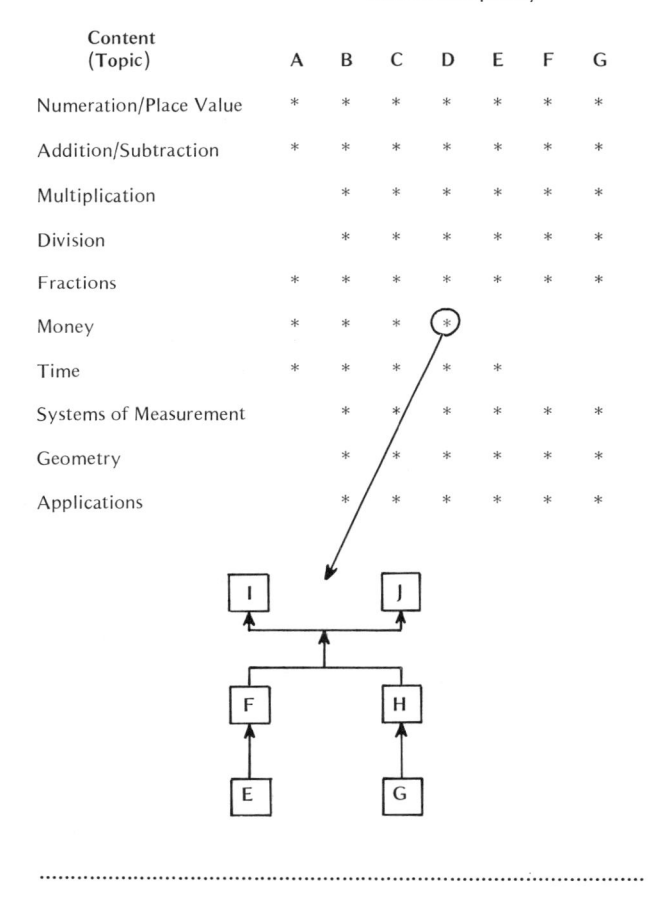

| Content (Topic) | A | B | C | D | E | F | G |
|---|---|---|---|---|---|---|---|
| Numeration/Place Value | * | * | * | * | * | * | * |
| Addition/Subtraction | * | * | * | * | * | * | * |
| Multiplication |   | * | * | * | * | * | * |
| Division |   | * | * | * | * | * | * |
| Fractions | * | * | * | * | * | * | * |
| Money | * | * | * | * |   |   |   |
| Time | * | * | * | * | * |   |   |
| Systems of Measurement |   | * | * | * | * | * | * |
| Geometry |   | * | * | * | * | * | * |
| Applications |   | * | * | * | * | * | * |

*Indicates a unit of instruction consisting of one or more instructional objectives.

## Figure 2

## Current IPI Testing and Instructional Procedure
## (Modified from Lindvall and Cox, 1969)

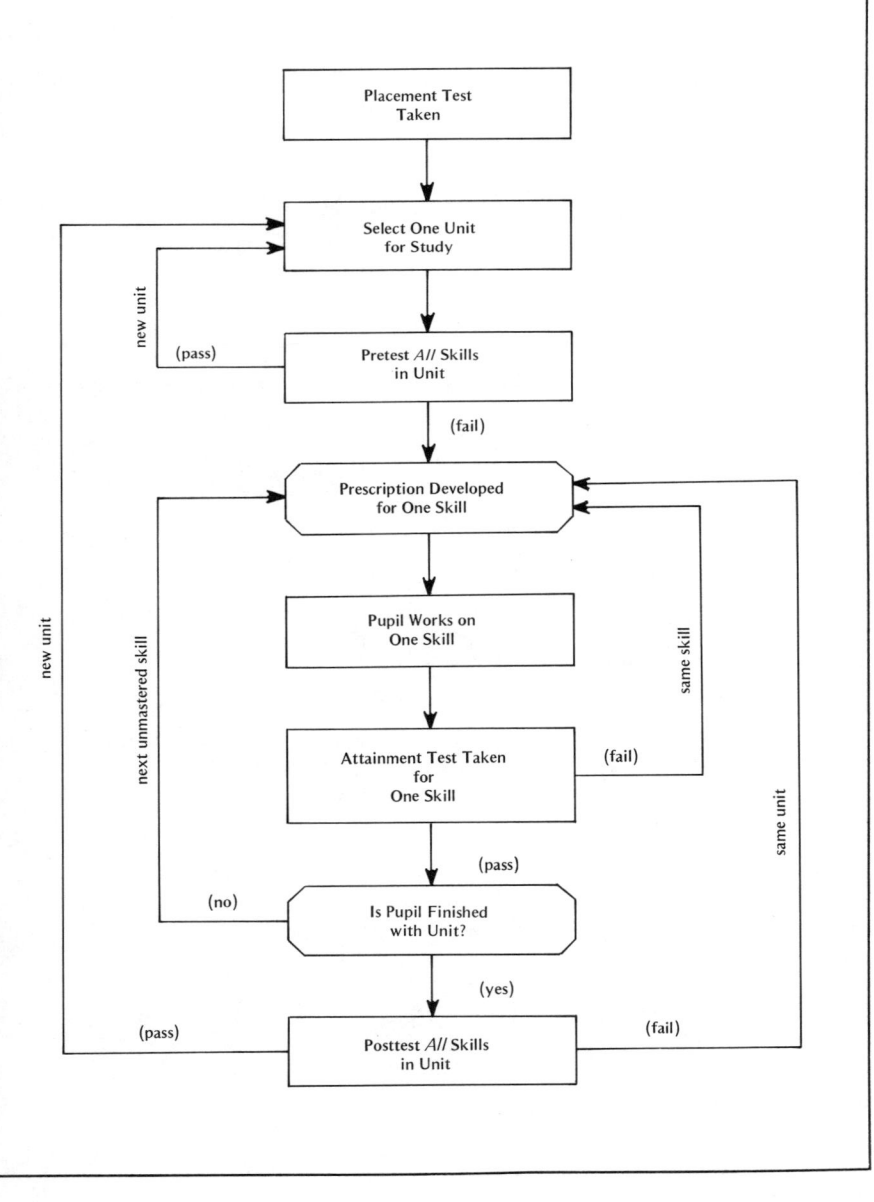

*Figure 3*

*Proposed Testing and Instructional Procedure*

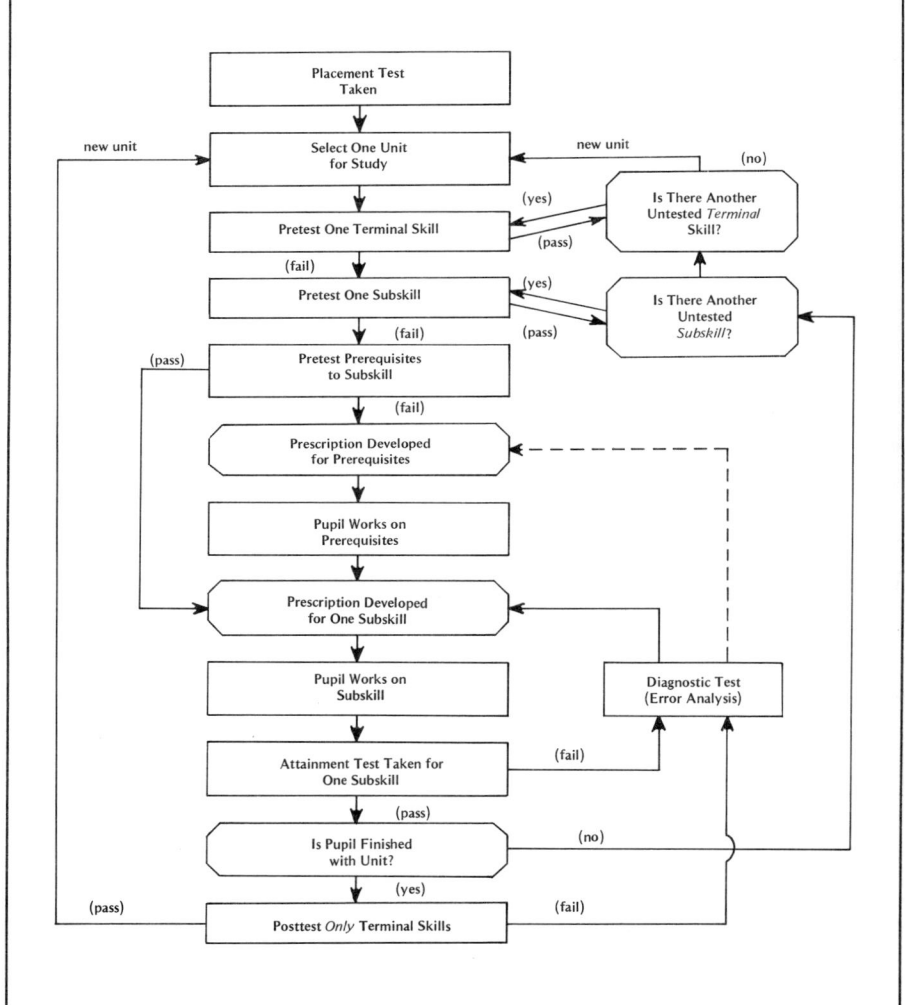

## Table 1

### Pupil Information Requirements in Adaptive Individualized Instruction

I. **Placement Information**
"Where should this pupil be located in the curricular sequence to begin his instruction?"
*Example*: Johnny should begin his studies at C-Level Addition, Objective 4.

II. **Diagnostic Information**
"What are the characteristics of the instruction that should be given this student so that he will be able to master the skill at which he was placed?"
*Examples*: Sue should review those C-Level skills related to regrouping before studying D-Level Subtraction Objective 4. Johnny regroups from hundreds to tens but does not change the hundreds digit accordingly. Review regrouping skills.

III. **Attainment Information**
"Has the student acquired the skill(s) on which he has been instructed?"
*Examples*: Jim has demonstrated mastery of D-Level Addition, Objective 5 by getting $\geq$ 85 percent of the items on the CET correct. Johnny has scored at or beyond the criterion level for all objectives in the C Subtraction Unit, except for Objective 3.

## The Technology of Adaptive Placement Testing

Let us consider the problem of placing a student into the learning sequence for a unit of instruction such as the one shown in the inset of Figure 1. (Decisions about what unit the learner should begin to study are discussed elsewhere, e.g., Cox and Boston, 1967.)

Each "box" in the learning sequence (or hierarchy) represents a behavioral objective. Each behavioral objective corresponds to one or more item forms. The items from these item forms allow the different aspects of the behavioral repertoire implied by an objective to be displayed. For example, variations in format, manner of responding, phrasing of the questions, etc., may be incorporated within a single instructional objective. Taken together, the item forms from all modes in the hierarchical structure of a unit form a domain of instructionally relevant tasks. (The size of a unit of instruction is arbitrary and based on considerations such as student motivation, and practical instruction considerations, such as available instructional time.)

In this context, domain-referenced testing increases the content validity of placement tests by (1) making the domain to be tested explicit and (2) allowing a systematic sampling plan to be developed for that domain.

Following the testing scheme illustrated in Figure 2, one must test all the objectives in a unit in order to make a placement decision. Since a single test item provides an unreliable basis on which to make a placement decision with respect to an objective, subtests need to be developed by generating several items from each item form. In a 15-objective unit, for example, a student would need to take 15 subtests, whether he needed them or not. Such a testing scheme is non-adaptive and time-consuming.

In an effort to better adapt *placement* testing to the individual learner, Ferguson (1970) and others (Ferguson and Hsu, 1971; Hsu and Carlson, 1972) have explored the use of a computer as a test administrator and decision-maker.

The decisions for which the testing procedure must provide information are (1) *what* objectives should be tested and (2) does the pupil have *mastery* or *non-mastery* of the objectives that are tested. A decision must be made about each objective. However, the procedure allows one to make these decisions without actually testing each objective, and it also minimizes the amount of testing for those that are tested. This is accomplished by means of a set of decision rules which combine the unique capabilities of the computer with both statistical logic and subject matter logic.

Decisions concerning mastery of an objective were made by employing the Wald (1947) sequential probability ratio. This statistical procedure allows the test length to vary from pupil to pupil. Each pupil is given only as many test items as are necessary to make a decision with respect to mastery criteria and within prespecified (theoretical) probabilities of misclassification.

Since the objectives can be organized into a learning hierarchy, the psychological structure can be employed as part of the decision-making procedure. This consideration results in a compound *branching rule*— that is, a rule for determining the *next* objective to be tested. Choice of the next objective on which a student is to be tested depends on whether he was declared a master or a non-master of the last objective and on his response pattern that lead to the decision.

Thus, testing began at an objective in the middle of the hierarchy and continued until the branching rule could not be satisfied. At that point, the objective tested was the proper location of the student with respect to the hierarchy. Untested skills could be assumed mastered or unmastered according to their position in the hierarchy and the student's response data. The over-all testing procedure results in a placement profile for the unit.

In order to use the computer to perform large-scale testing for an entire curriculum it is necessary to have it actually generate the test items. Large-scale, practical programs of this kind have not yet been developed, but they represent a promising area of application of the computer to instruction.

## The Technology of Diagnostic Testing

The problem of using norm-referenced aptitude measures to match learners with methods and materials will not be discussed in this chapter. Instead we will describe how the technology of computer-based testing has been used to clarify the patterns of strength and weakness in an individual's idiosyncratic repertoire for purposes of remediation.

The practical problem is this: Sometimes the pre-arranged instructional materials in an instructional program, for which a system of placement and attainment tests has been designed already, do not effectively teach an individual student. His behavior is too idiosyncratic even for an adaptive program of instruction. A special prescription needs to be written. For this purpose, item forms can be formulated on the basis of empirical evidence of learning difficulties and misunderstandings together with a theoretical analysis of the cognitive processes underlying task performance. Using such item forms, test items can be generated which will aid in identifying classes of tasks for which identifiable response patterns suggest similar underlying cognitive processes. If a profile can be developed for a learner, indicating the classes of tasks with which he has difficulty, then appropriate remedial materials may be prescribed.

Domain-referenced testing has been used successfully in this kind of diagnostic testing in a computer-assisted testing project at the

Learning Research and Development Center. The application has been in the area of elementary school arithmetic (Hsu and Carlson, 1972). A single objective of the curriculum was defined by several item forms. Each item form was so developed that the problem generated from it tended to elicit particular types of errors if not answered correctly. For example, if an objective was: "Multiply a three-digit number by a three-digit number using the multiplication algorithm," then aspects such as carrying or non-carrying, the magnitude of the carry, the appearance of zero in the factors and the place value from which the carry occurred served to define item-form cells that specified clusters of items over which common types of errors might appear.

If the objective as a whole was not mastered, then the computer was programmed to print out a description of the clusters of items the student missed along with the pupil's score. Using procedures similar to those provided by the Dade County Study of arithmetic errors (Nesbit, 1966), the teacher may then be able to tailor instruction to the individual. (The Dade County Study is useful in delineating the type of errors pupils frequently make and the types of arithmetic problems frequently associated with these errors. Item forms can be developed on the basis of these data.)

This type of diagnostic test was integrated into a unit pretesting and posttesting scheme. The possibility of developing item forms which generate classes of items that would allow consistent types of erroneous responses to be displayed has not been well explored for areas outside of mathematics. However, defining domains of items along the lines of probable types of erroneous responses provides a clear line of research having payoff in the daily instructional decision-making in the classroom.

## Attainment Testing: Reporting Progress
## and Grading Students

Under the best of circumstances, grading students is a controversial issue subject to much misinterpretation. However, if assessment of pupil achievement can be referenced to a defined and public domain of instructionally relevant tasks, much of the "emotion" associated with grading may be relieved. It is not our purpose to fully discuss all aspects of grading and their ramifications, serious as these may be Rather, we seek briefly to describe a domain-referenced pupil-progress reporting system that appears to be consistent with the approach to instruction and testing which we have outlined so far.

In the elementary school, progress reports communicate to pupils, parents and teachers (a) the skills and knowledge acquired, (b) the growth or progress during a given period of time and (c) comparisons of the achievement of comparable groups of pupils having comparable instruction (Terwilliger, 1971). If domains of instructionally relevant tasks are keyed to the curriculum, then reporting pupil progress in individualized instruction can be relatively straightforward. Numbered boxes on a report card represent units of the curriculum which have been arranged in a prerequisite sequence. At the end of each marking period, the teacher marks an "X" in the boxes for the unit (s) the pupil has mastered during that marking period. A numeral written next to the "X" indicates the marking period (1, 2, 3, 4). A slash ("/") indicates the unit on which the learner is currently receiving instruction.

A simple list of skills mastered may not be sufficient in a report card of this kind. Parents need to know the hierarchical structure of the curriculum and the domain of tasks implied by the units of instruction to interpret their child's progress.

Parents often want to have comparative information about their child's progress, as well as information about his performance alone. This can be incorporated into the pupil's progress report also. One type of information concerns the grade level at which the particular unit of the curriculum is typically learned by pupils at a given school (Millman, 1970). Thus, a statement, such as, "Unit 10 is typically learned by the end of first grade," allows the individual pupil's progress in any given marking period to be given a comparative interpretation. Another piece of information that might be provided with the pupil progress report is the average number of school days (math periods) the class of pupils takes to master each unit. Since units vary in difficulty, this may help to explain why one pupil mastered three units while the neighbor's child mastered five units.

Other problems enter into comparative interpretation of pupil progress in this context. We have already mentioned the fact that some units of the curriculum are more difficult (i.e., take a longer time to complete) than others. Thus, students who are not studying comparable parts of the curriculum cannot be compared with respect to rate of progress. Further, if the instruction is individualized and adaptive, pupils in a given classroom (grade or age) will be placed at different points in the learning sequence. Thus, comparisons of progress become subject to misinterpretation. One suggestion is to report comparative data for pupils who were similarly placed at the beginning of the school year. Table 2 shows a hypothetical example of such supplementary comparative data. For each marking period, the ID number of the highest, median and lowest unit mastered in the group is shown. The data are based on the group of children who were initially placed in units 1, 2 or 3. Thus, of all the students who began the school year in units 1, 2 or 3, the fastest student had completed unit 15 at the end of the third marking period, the median or "typical" student had completed unit 11 and the slowest student had completed unit 7. Other averages and statistical summaries can be reported as well, such as, the average number of units of the curriculum a given group completed during a marking period.

Many other types of "grading" systems are possible, of course. Suggestions such as those of Millman (1970), Bloom, Hastings and Madaus (1971) or Airasian and Madaus (1972) can be adapted to a domain-referenced achievement testing system.

*Table 2*

*Example of Norm-Referenced Data for a Domain-Referenced Pupil Progress Report*

Summary Data for Students with Initial Placement in Units 1, 2 or 3

|  | Marking Period ||||
| --- | --- | --- | --- | --- |
|  | 1 | 2 | 3 | 4 |
| Highest Unit Mastered | 5 | 11 | 15 |  |
| Median Unit Mastered | 3 | 8 | 11 |  |
| Lowest Unit Mastered | 2 | 5 | 7 |  |
| Average Number of Units Mastered This Period | 3 | 2 | 3 |  |

## Conclusion

We have attempted to illustrate how domain-referenced testing might be used in an adaptive and individualized system of instruction. Our main theme is that measurement and instruction should be integrated into a decision-making context. This implies that the underlying psychological structure of the curriculum be the basis for the development and use of domains of test tasks providing information for instructional decision-making.

Our examples have stemmed from our association with elementary school arithmetic curricula. We hope that they can be extended to other curricular areas and feel confident that this can be accomplished. The techniques used in domain-referenced test development have important implications for all instructional areas. They make explicit the classes of tasks that the learner is required to master. The analysis required facilitates an understanding of the processes involved in performing complex school-related tasks.

## References

Airasian, P.W. and G.F. Madaus. Criterion-Referenced Testing in the Classroom. *Measurement in Education*, 1972, *3* (4).

Bloom, B.S., T.M. Hastings and G.F. Madaus. *Handbook on Formative and Summative Evaluation of Student Learning*. New York: McGraw-Hill, 1971.

Cox, R. and M.E. Boston. Diagnosis of Pupil Achievement in the Individually Prescribed Instruction Project. Pittsburgh: Learning Research and Development Center, University of Pittsburgh, 1967.

Cronbach, L.J. and R.E. Snow. Individual Differences in Learning Ability as a Function of Instructional Variables: Final Report. Stanford, California: Stanford University, School of Education, 1969.

Ferguson, R.L. A Model for Computer-Assisted Criterion-Referenced Measurement. *Education*, 1970, *81*, 25-31.

Ferguson, R. and T.C. Hsu. The Application of Item Generators for Individualizing Mathematics Testing and Instruction. Pittsburgh: Learning Research and Development Center, University of Pittsburgh, 1971.

Glaser, R. Individuals and Learning: The New Aptitudes. *Educational Researcher, 1* (6), 1972, 5-13.

Glaser, R. and A.J. Nitko. Measurement in Learning and Instruction. In R.L. Thorndike (Ed.) *Educational Measurement* (Second Edition). Washington, D.C.: American Council on Education, 1971.

Hsu, T.C. and M. Carlson. Computer-Assisted Achievement Testing. Pittsburgh: Learning Research and Development Center, University of Pittsburgh, 1972.

Lindvall, C.M. and J.O. Bolvin. Programmed Instruction in the Schools: An

Application of Programming Principles in "Individually Prescribed Instruction." In P. Lange (Ed.) *Programmed Instruction, Sixty-sixth Yearbook, Part II.* Chicago: National Society for the Study of Education, 1967, 217-254.

Lindvall, C.M. and R.C. Cox. The Role of Evaluation in Programs for Individualized Instruction. In *Sixty-eighth Yearbook of the National Society for the Study of Education, Part II.* Chicago: NSSE, 1969, 156-188.

Millman, J. Reporting Student Progress: A Case for a Criterion-Referenced Marking System. *Phi Delta Kappan*, December 1970, 226-230.

Nesbit, M.Y. The CHILD program: Computer Help in Learning Diagnosis of Arithmetic Scores. Miami: Dade County Board of Public Instruction, 1966.

Terwilliger, J.S. *Assigning Grades to Students.* Glenview, Illinois: Scott, Foresman and Company, 1971.

Wald, A. *Sequential Analysis.* New York: Wiley, 1947.

# Tracking Behavioral Growth: Day-to-Day Measures of Frequency Over Domains of Performance

Ann Dell Duncan

Domain-referenced testing wears many hats. Its structural simplicity allows it to be merged with other areas of interest, amplifying the total effect. My area of interest is to study ways to help people more effectively guide themselves and support each other. Humane behaviorism is my profession and the methods of operant-behavior analysis are my tools (Duncan, Hively and Spence, 1974). The intent of this chapter is to show how domain-referenced testing clarifies and facilitates this work. By combining the methods of precise personal management (PPM) with those of domain-referenced testing (DRT) we are developing a new approach to educational measurement called Participatory Evaluation (Hively and Duncan, 1972). The basic ingredients of Participatory Evaluation are frequency-of-response measures and time series analysis, applied to behavioral domains. Its purpose is the facilitation of behavior change.

Our early work in educational "behavior modification" consisted of helping teachers eliminate children's behaviors considered obnoxious in the classroom. This work was often temporarily successful but had little lasting effect. We turned to teaching people how to change

**Ann Dell Duncan** formerly at the University of Minnesota, Minneapolis, is now at Spaulding Youth Center, Tilton, New Hampshire.

themselves in a hope for more permanence (Duncan, 1969). Where previously our goal was causing children to change, it has shifted to showing teachers and children how to change themselves. In other words, PPM is the self-application of basic behavioral principles. We believe that the future of applied behavior analysis in education lies in this direction. Most people committed to long-term behavior growth ascribe to the ultimate goals of personal and reciprocal management. Thus, all practitioners of behavioral management in education should be working to put themselves out of business.

**Important Ingredients of PPM**

PPM combines the descriptive tools of behavior analysis with a standard but non-technical language and a graphic method of data representation (the Standard Behavior Chart) specifically designed to facilitate precision communication among teachers and learners (Pennypacker, Koenig and Lindsley, 1972). The tools are:

(1) frequency of occurrence of pinpointed behavioral episodes as the fundamental measure;
(2) time series analysis as the measurement model; and
(3) reinforcement theory as the principal guide to finding ways to change.

An example of the tools at work may be seen in Arlene R's case of self doubts. Arlene is a resource teacher who works with children and teachers every day. She found herself plagued by self doubts to the point where she decided to count the frequency of their occurrence and see how serious a problem they really were.

She recorded every instance of self doubt, little or big, fleeting or long. For the first eight days, she averaged 10 a day. She discovered, by looking at the recorded data, that self doubts were not as frequent on weekends as they were during the week. When she went on vacation, she enjoyed a respite from self doubting, even though the trend was moving back up as she came closer to going back to school. In the middle of April, Arlene decided on a specific change procedure drawn from her knowledge of reinforcement principles: she wrote each thought down as it occurred and listed the circumstances surrounding it. She also tried to write down an objective solution to each dilemma and act on it. The average frequency of self doubts for the remainder of the project was one per day, a comfort level she could live with.

This project exemplifies several of the important characteristics of

*Tracking Behavioral Growth* 125

PPM: (1) self selection of a behavior to study; (2) selection of the behavior from an important area of personal concern; (3) precise recording and graphic display of the daily data leading to: (4) discoveries from the chart (weekend effects and impact of vacation), followed by: (5) systematic efforts to change the frequency of the behavior until a comfort level is reached.

## Important Ingredients of DRT

Learning is primarily an exchange: from someone who knows something to someone who does not. All the competencies needed by today's young people may not be easy to define, but some people have them and others need to learn them.

The logic of domain-referenced testing enables an educational "smithy" to define and communicate accurately the domains of competency he wishes to convey to an apprentice. Likewise, DRT provides the apprentice with a way to confirm the competencies he believes he has attained and to present himself for certification to his tutor and to other smithies; to debate, if necessary, what competencies are best for what purposes, and to be an active participant in the educational process.

The activity of constructing a domain-referenced testing system produces something more significant than an evaluation instrument. The emphasis it places on procedures for generating curricular items and clarifying the underlying organization of the subject matter provides a basis for agreement among teachers, and between teachers and students about their shared educational goals.

With domain-referenced testing we can merge the joys of teaching and the discoveries from testing. We no longer have to be adversaries of our students. We can join with them in learning new ways to present curriculum, facilitate self-discovery, and project future learning.

## What Behavior Analysis Needs from
## Domain-Referenced Testing

When working with productive learning, the behavior analyst is inevitably led to the problem of measuring frequencies of behaviors over domains. Such pinpoints as "adding two-digit numbers," "reading single words aloud correctly" or "answering comprehension questions" all imply a process of sampling from a domain. Each pinpoint needs to be referenced in a way that makes sense to a commonly agreed-upon repertoire or response class.

Behavior analysts have in the past tended to focus on small pieces of behavior and to ignore their relationship to larger domains. One of the criticisms reasonably leveled at this kind of measurement is its lack of generalizability. Does learning to draw straight lines at 10 per minute have any connection with a child's ultimate goal of reading? Such questions lead us directly into learning hierarchies and domain definitions (Rosner, 1973).

Allen F. tutored a boy named John. John's problem was that he did not know how to read very well—and he did not like reading almost as much as he did not know how to read. Allen decided to try a number of high interest books with John to see if he could find some answers to such questions as: Could John read a high interest reader? Would he get faster the more books he read? Was there any way of determining his motivation from the way he read the books? John could read, and he read a little faster as he went through the seven different books. The over-all growth was not dramatic but it was an encouraging acceleration of five percent better per week. As we would expect, John's frequency dropped each time he left an old familiar book and started on a new one.

But was John really learning to read more fluently? The upward trends within each book were obvious: John was catching on to the vocabulary and style of each different writer, but did the over-all trend across books imply a general increase in reading fluency? Maybe the books just happened to get easier. The way to avoid that uncertainty would be to define a broader domain of reading materials (perhaps through the use of readability formulas and library catalogue lists) and allow John and his classmates to test themselves periodically on samples drawn from it.

**Time Series Analysis and DRT**

The measurement strategy utilized by Allen in working with John differs from those one usually expects to encounter in education. Usually, "tests" are given only once or twice. Few teachers and students, unless they have been taught the technology of Precision Teaching (Lindsley, 1971), make decisions on the basis of daily performance measures, charted so that the teacher can notice acceleration or deceleration of specific behaviors (trends). With the advent of domain-referenced testing, multiple-shot measurement is becoming a more frequent practice.

One-shot administrations of domain-referenced tests are used to describe populations and to make curriculum-placement decisions:
- "the domain score for our 6th graders on decimal division was only 50 percent: we should improve teaching in that area."
- "Maria correctly answered 80 percent of the items from the decimal division domain: she should be encouraged to go on to percentages."

Two-shot administrations (the typical pre-post tests) are used to show the effects of specific "treatments": "on October 5, Maria's pretest domain score for decimal division was 50 percent; on November 8, after working on the decimals unit, her posttest score was 80 percent: the unit was probably helpful to Maria."

Two-shot administrations are only useful in a deductive-prescriptive model of evaluation. If variables that may influence performance have been predicted on the basis of some theory, then analysis of variance in the pre-post test design can be used to see how significant their effects really were. Then, if they seem to have worked for Maria (and her classmates) they can be used again on next year's students, providing those students learn in the same way as Maria.

But what if they do not work for Maria? By the time we usually posttest, we have waited too long to help her effectively. And what if we do not know in advance the things that are most likely to facilitate or inhibit Maria's growth? To track Maria and help her more systematically, we must use multiple-shot test administrations.

Multiple-shot administrations are used to find effective changes by the inductive method. The main reason for frequent measurement is to project the future rate of change in a repertoire and take action to help it change. How rapidly is Maria learning to read? Has she reached a plateau with the present materials? Would vocabulary drill help? These are questions answerable only by time-series analysis—and time-series analysis relies on DRT. It does not make sense to give the same norm-referenced test over and over again: there is no way to generate a large number of parallel forms. However, multiple samples from a reading domain may be scheduled to show trends in growth and to provide a basis for future projection.

Time-series analysis is not new, but its use in educational

decision-making is rare. (A good, recent explication of time-series analysis procedures and their connection to educational evaluation may be found in Glass, Willson and Gottman, 1972). Dow-Jones uses time-series analysis because they need the information to make economic projections about the future. They need a base to describe today's behavior and predict what is coming tomorrow. Perhaps time-series analysis is not as widely used in education because deciding what is best for our children does not affect us as quickly or as sharply as deciding whether to buy or sell a stock. For some it may seem wasteful or expensive to measure so frequently in education. But when we launch spacecraft toward the moon, measures are taken continuously on the behaviors of the men as well as the ship. Constant monitoring allows changes to be introduced at propitious times as well as predictions to be made about the coming events. If we were to launch 5000 similar craft, it might not be so important to continuously monitor and adjust. The chances of a few arriving at the moon might be sufficiently large that a pretest-posttest design would do. The analogy to education is clear: is each child a spacecraft needing careful tending—or are some expendable?

For one- and two-shot measures, "error variance" is theoretically handled (as described in Millman's chapter) by the standard error of proportions based on the assumption of a binomial distribution. For multiple measures we can do better than that. Variation can be empirically determined by the observed bounce around a trend-projection line. The binomial theorem generally overestimates the observed variation.

**Frequency Measures and DRT**

In DRT the basic idea is to estimate the probability of correct responses to a defined domain of stimuli. There are two classic ways to estimate this probability: (1) the proportion of correct answers in a sample (the measure emphasized by the other authors in this book) and (2) the frequency of correct responses per unit time when the learner is presented with a series of stimuli and is free to respond to each or skip to the next. Proportion correct is a measure of accuracy. Frequency correct is a measure of fluency. We do not know much yet about how these two estimates are related but we can keep track of both. Keeping track of both may provide us with much more sensitive descriptions of the effects of curricula, motivating conditions and their interaction with individual learning styles than are provided by measures of accuracy alone (Spence, 1973).

A nice illustration of the relationship between fluency and accuracy is provided by a time-series record of reading behavior gathered through the Reading Exchange of the Psycho-Educational Center at the University of Minnesota. Seven-year-old Connie, with a little help from her mother, read aloud each day for one minute from the *Dear Abby* column of the local newspaper. Connie counted the number of words she read correctly (hits), words she read incorrectly (misses) and words she did not attempt to read (skips). In the beginning her frequency of hits was relatively low, while skips and misses were high. Soon, however, Connie stopped skipping and began to guess more often: her misses accelerated and skips decelerated, while the frequency of hits remained about the same. When Connie started working with a tutor, hits began to accelerate and misses began to decelerate at a slow but steady rate. (See Figures 1 and 2.)

From the data collected, two interesting things emerge: (1) The proportion correct is approaching a ceiling so that we will not be able to detect much more growth by looking only at it. However, (2) the frequency of hits still has plenty of room to grow (an adult can read comfortably aloud from *Dear Abby* at a frequency of about 200 words per minute). Connie is a fairly accurate but not very fluent reader.

*Dear Abby* is an approximate domain. Although the vocabulary and structure of the daily column are fairly constant from week to week, there are no precise generative rules governing the production of test materials. However, the same daily one-minute sample can be taken from more precisely defined domains. For example, we can present a learner with a series of randomly generated mathematics problems and let him answer or skip over as many as he likes in a fixed period of time. The CAM procedure described by Rabehl and Sension, this book, could easily be adapted to this measurement strategy.

In general, we suspect that if you give the learner freedom to select the items to which he wishes to respond, you will obtain more sensitive measures of the acquisition process than if you present him with a fixed, arbitrarily chosen sample. In "power tests," frequency is lost and in "speed tests" frequency is arbitrarily converted to proportion. In both cases we may be throwing away our most sensitive measures.

## Figure 1

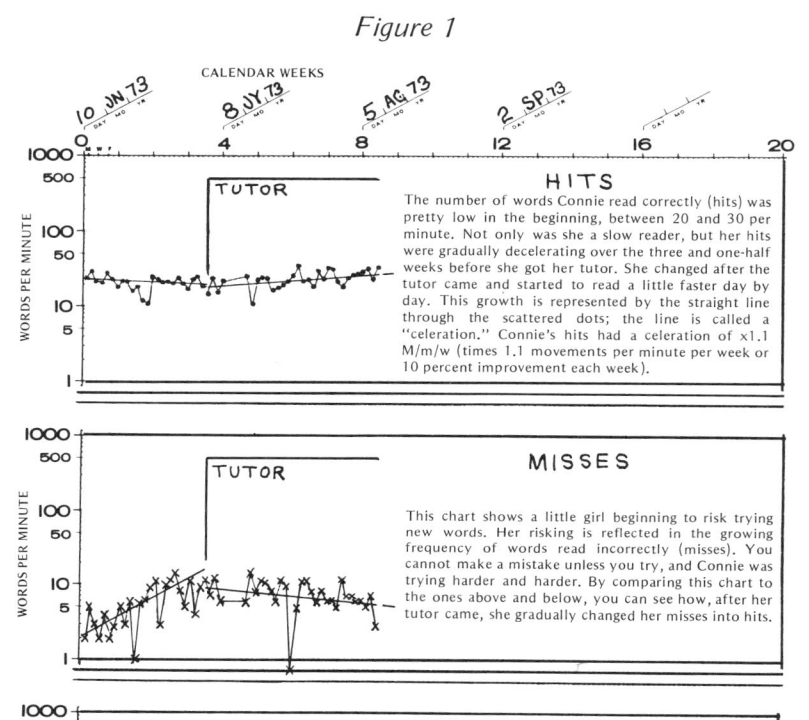

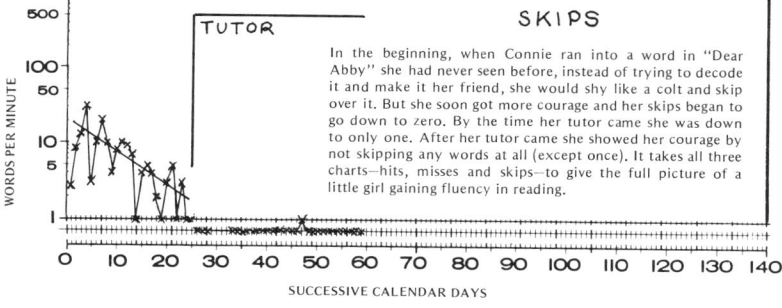

### HITS

The number of words Connie read correctly (hits) was pretty low in the beginning, between 20 and 30 per minute. Not only was she a slow reader, but her hits were gradually decelerating over the three and one-half weeks before she got her tutor. She changed after the tutor came and started to read a little faster day by day. This growth is represented by the straight line through the scattered dots; the line is called a "celeration." Connie's hits had a celeration of x1.1 M/m/w (times 1.1 movements per minute per week or 10 percent improvement each week).

### MISSES

This chart shows a little girl beginning to risk trying new words. Her risking is reflected in the growing frequency of words read incorrectly (misses). You cannot make a mistake unless you try, and Connie was trying harder and harder. By comparing this chart to the ones above and below, you can see how, after her tutor came, she gradually changed her misses into hits.

### SKIPS

In the beginning, when Connie ran into a word in "Dear Abby" she had never seen before, instead of trying to decode it and make it her friend, she would shy like a colt and skip over it. But she soon got more courage and her skips began to go down to zero. By the time her tutor came she was down to only one. After her tutor came she showed her courage by not skipping any words at all (except once). It takes all three charts—hits, misses and skips—to give the full picture of a little girl gaining fluency in reading.

**CONNIE'S READING FLUENCY CHARTS**

Connie read aloud out of the "Dear Abby" column of the Minneapolis Tribune. Her mother helped her count the words she read correctly (hits), words she mispronounced (misses), and words she did not try to read (skips). They put the dots or "x's" for her daily performance on the Standard Behavior Chart (SBC).

Shown above are abbreviated versions of the SBC. The three actual charts that Connie used are cropped off at the one word-per-minute line and pasted together so that you can readily glance from one chart to another and see the progress in fluency (hits compared with skips), accuracy (hits compared with misses) and risking (misses compared with skips).

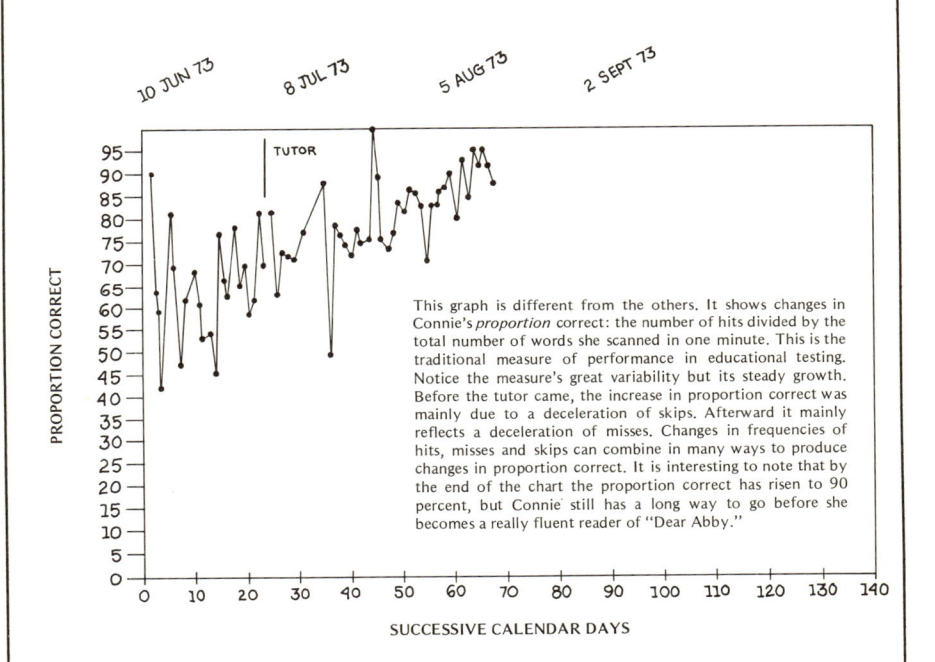

## Figure 2

[Chart: PROPORTION CORRECT (y-axis, 0–95) vs. SUCCESSIVE CALENDAR DAYS (x-axis, 0–140), with date markers at 10 JUN 73, 8 JUL 73, 5 AUG 73, 2 SEPT 73, and a "TUTOR" annotation.]

This graph is different from the others. It shows changes in Connie's *proportion* correct: the number of hits divided by the total number of words she scanned in one minute. This is the traditional measure of performance in educational testing. Notice the measure's great variability but its steady growth. Before the tutor came, the increase in proportion correct was mainly due to a deceleration of skips. Afterward it mainly reflects a deceleration of misses. Changes in frequencies of hits, misses and skips can combine in many ways to produce changes in proportion correct. It is interesting to note that by the end of the chart the proportion correct has risen to 90 percent, but Connie still has a long way to go before she becomes a really fluent reader of "Dear Abby."

### CONNIE'S PROPORTION CORRECT CHART

#### A Note About the Standard Behavior Chart

The information presented in Figure 1 was collected by a child herself, with a little help from a few adults in such things as keeping time, counting up the words, putting the dots on the charts (in the beginning) and being supportive to the entire information-seeking project. It takes about one minute to do the reading, one minute to put the dots on the charts, and three minutes to compare the three charts. So for a cost of five minutes a day, parent, child, teacher and administrator can have daily measures of fluency, accuracy and risk taking in reading, both for individuals and for entire classrooms. The charts allow both the child and the helping adults to see long-run progress and feel rewarded by the results. This is possible because the information can be collected and presented in a convenient, standardized form. That is the purpose of the Standard Behavior Chart: it is designed to maximize communication about human behavior.

To learn more about the Standard Behavior Chart and the logic behind using a multiply-divide (semi-logarithmic) chart to picture changes in behavior frequencies, see Pennypacker *et al.*, 1973.

If there is anything we have learned from our work with behavior analysis it is that frequency of response is a prime measure of motivation. This may give us a key to generalizing beyond performance in an artificial domain to the abstract universe. In the long run we are interested not only in how fluently and accurately Connie reads from *Dear Abby* but also in how fluently and accurately she reads throughout her daily life. If we give Connie the tools for precise personal recording, she may be able to track for herself the total number of hits, misses and skips in all her reading throughout her normal day. Such measures reflect not only Connie's ability but also her interest. This might let us find out what we would really like to know: how much does she read, what kinds of things does she read and how accurately does she do it? By merging the techniques of precise personal management with the techniques of domain-referenced testing, we may be able to provide Connie with the skills she needs to track this growth and present it to other people for their evaluation and assistance. That is the basic idea behind Participatory Evaluation.

In education, people who have repertoires of competence arrange conditions to help youngsters meet the future. In doing this they say to the learner, "These are the things that were important for us, they should be important to you." With Participatory Evaluation, we may now find out to what extent those repertoires are also important to the learners. In this way education may move out of the past and into the present. With precision, reciprocity and cooperation, we may all be better prepared to meet the future.

## References

Duncan, A.D. Self-Application of Behavior Modification Techniques by Teen-Agers. *Adolescence*, 1969, 6, 541-556.

Duncan, A.D., W. Hively and I. Spence. *Precise Personal Management and Precision Teaching: A Handbook for Humane Behaviorists.* New York: David McKay, 1974.

Glass, G.V., V.L. Willson, and J.M. Gottman. *Design and Analysis of Time Series Experiments.* Laboratory for Research in Education, University of Colorado, 1972.

Hively, W. and A.D. Duncan. Participatory Evaluation. Proposal submitted to the National Study of School Evaluation, June 1972.

Lindsley, O.R. Precision Teaching in Perspective: An Interview with O.R. Lindsley. *Teaching Exceptional Children*, Spring 1971.

Pennypacker, H.S., C.H. Koenig and O.R. Lindsley. *Handbook of the Standard Behavior Chart.* Precision Media (Box 3222, Kansas City, Kansas 66103), 1972.

Rosner, J. Testing for Teaching in an Adaptive Educational Environment. Learning Research and Development Center, University of Pittsburgh, 1973.

Spence, I. The View of a Psychologist. In C. Gattegno (Ed.) *An Experimental School.* New York: Educational Solutions, 1973.

# PART THREE

# PERSPECTIVES

# Some Comments

Wells Hively

As this book's editor, I find both pleasure and concern in its contents. The pleasure comes from contrasting the contributions by authors who, although they have had little direct contact with one another, share many common themes. The concern has to do with whether we have communicated those themes effectively to you, the reader. If our task has been done well, these contents should provide new perspectives on your own endeavors. To that end I will briefly discuss the chapters, emphasizing comparisons and contrasts, and then try to tie together some threads that weave throughout.

## Notes on the Chapters
*Beyond Objectives*

From Eva L. Baker I learned a good deal about the process of generating domains. Eva's approach is deductive: she starts with carefully stated behavioral objectives and then builds up domains to represent them. Mine is inductive: I build up domains by transforming and generalizing prototypical items or tasks, and then I give the domains descriptive names afterward. Clearly we ought to work in both directions. Eva's chapter provides a helpful bridge between the domain-referencing technology I know (Hively *et al.*, 1973) and the "behavioral objectives approach" associated with writers like Mager (1962).

*Sampling Plans for Domain-Referenced Tests*

Jason Millman's chapter (for those willing to pause a minute and study the equations) is the best introduction I have yet seen to the mathematical model underlying DRT. His references solidly point the way to the necessary background literature for those who want to delve further into the model. (Ann Dell Duncan's sketch of the time-series analysis applications of DRT nicely supplements Millman's chapter and highlights an area in which some exciting work is unfolding.)

*Domains and Instructional Accountability*

George J. Rabehl and Donald B. Sension have shown DRT actually put to work in schools to provide data for their day-to-day operation. The authors' low key, common sense approach is persuasive, and I look forward to further reports of CAM and other DRT approaches to on-going evaluation of school programs.

*Content, Items, Decisions—*
*Program and Product Evaluation*

The ambitious, theoretical chapters by Donald M. Miller and Thomas J. Johnson have many elements in common—not surprisingly, since both are heavily involved in large-scale practical applications. (Each might profit from utilizing in their over-all designs some of the specific domain-generation techniques described by Eva Baker.) The big pictures that they paint are very useful, but I occasionally find myself saying, "Oops, that looks pretty formidable." The trick is to find practical procedures which approximate the models presented by Miller and Johnson, but which can be implemented within brief periods of time. If assessments or program evaluations cannot go from the planning phase to the data collection phase within a year, they probably will be of little practical use.

*Teacher Evaluation and*
*Domain-Referenced Measurement*

W. James Popham has written a characteristically readable and thought-provoking chapter. I share his concern about the fairness of domains: behavioral competencies must be well-defined and mutually agreeable if they are to serve as the basis for teacher evaluation.

# Some Comments

### Performance Contracting Experiments

Performance contracting may have dropped out of the news, but the comprehensive and thoughtful chapter by Guilbert C. Hentschke and Donald M. Levine makes several points which have far broader implications. The variables they discuss are, of course, equally applicable to Popham's problem.

### Placement, Diagnosis and Attainment

As time goes on, I find myself losing faith in the classical IPI system—wherein learners are tested, placed in a learning hierarchy and then moved on from unit to unit as a result of decision rules about their levels of competency in each subskill. But the chapter by Anthony J. Nitko and Tse-Chi Hsu shows clearly how DRT underlies the IPI model. With people like Nitko, Lauren Resnick and Jerome Rosner doing the exploring, it will be interesting to see what the next evolution of the University of Pittsburgh model will look like.

### Tracking Behavioral Growth

The chapter by Ann Dell Duncan is a synthesis of things Ann and I have recently learned from each other. We find ourselves looking for ways to help learners define and track performance in their own chosen domains, rather than to guide them through a predefined instructional system. Eventually the ingredients of Participatory Evaluation will probably be melded with those of IPI.

## Important Threads

Many people have written about how formal conceptual models guide our work. Thomas Kuhn (1962) calls these "paradigms" and Kenneth Boulding (1961) calls them "images." In education, the "image" of NRT has dominated our actions for a long time. My main purpose in this book has been to clarify an alternative image. The image of domain-referenced testing is that of a *repertoire* of behavior. Its associates are performance generalization, instructional transfer, subject matter structure and educational technology. The problems of specifying important classes of situations, and the classes of responses appropriate to them, to serve as targets for instruction is the problem of DRT.

With this image in mind, different people may use DRT in a variety of diverse applications, appropriate to different practical

purposes. There is no one, standard way to do domain-referenced testing. However, there are two basic characteristics that distinguish all applications and which are worth emphasizing:
1. Items may never be added to, or removed from, a domain on the basis of their difficulties or their correlations with other items. The formal characteristics of an item, independent of students' responses to it, are what determine its inclusion or exclusion. Items are classed together to form domains on the basis of similarities in their stimuli and responses.
2. In a domain-referenced testing system, scores are always estimates of the probability that an individual (or group) will respond similarly to other items. As Millman and Duncan have explained, such estimates are either proportions or frequencies.

With these two basic characteristics in mind, we can see that there may be many degrees of completeness in the specification of domains. A test that consists of a list of objectives with one item keyed to each objective may be properly called a domain-referenced test, so long as we clearly recognize that there is only one item in each sub-domain. However, the inference from the item score to the domain score is primitive: it only tells you about the probability that the students will respond correctly to that same item if you present it again.

If you want a stronger inference, you can construct more items for each objective, and then you can sample some of them and estimate the probability that the individual or group will respond correctly to the others. In this way, domains can be built up, little by little, by adding more and more items, until the range of representative instances is judged to be adequate. That is the only difference between a domain-referenced test and an objective-referenced test. The strength of the inference depends on the representativeness of the set of items associated with each objective.

In the same sense, a criterion-referenced test is also a domain-referenced test. Robert Glaser's chapter in Popham's collection (1971) does a good job of linking criterion-referenced testing to the idea of a domain:

> A criterion-referenced test is one that is deliberately constructed to yield measurements that are directly interpretable in terms of the specified performance standards. Performance standards are generally specified by defining a class or

## Some Comments 141

domain of tasks that should be performed by the individual. Measurements are taken on representative samples of tasks drawn from this domain and such measurements are referenced directly to this domain for each individual measure.

An approximate domain is better than none. So long as we keep the image in mind we can continually improve the domains associated with the instructional objectives. For practical purposes we may start with representative "item pools" and sophisticated item generation procedures may evolve naturally.

## Some Technicalities

Both Millman and Nitko take me to task for my definitions of reliability and validity for domain-referenced testing systems. The definitions *are* slightly different from our usual definitions of content and criterion validity. But I still think they are more useful definitions, and thus, here is a quick review of the model.

In the accompanying figure the large box outlined in wavy lines represents an idealized repertoire of real-world behavior. I have outlined it in wavy lines to suggest that it is *never* well-defined. All we can do is collect examples of the kinds of behavior it contains through field surveys and interviews of experts. The smaller hard-edged box represents a concrete domain of items defining a "nuclear" repertoire that is thought (by the people who defined it) to represent the essentials of the behaviors needed to perform well in the abstract universe. It has hard edges because it is an actual domain of well-defined test situations. The tiny box at the bottom represents a specific sample of items drawn from the concrete domain. To me the relationship between the two hard-edged boxes requires one kind of inference, while the relationship between the hard-edged box and the soft-edged box requires a different kind. The first I would prefer to call reliability. It has to do with the variation in proportions or frequencies obtained from parallel samples. The second has to do with validity, and it is based on correlations among a variety of measures, linking performance in the concrete domain to performance in the abstract universe. (See Figure 1.)

As Millman and Nitko point out, the operations which I wish to call reliability are called by many testing experts "content validity," while the other operations are called "criterion validity." Perhaps it is best to let future usage decide. However, it is important to underline

*Figure 1*

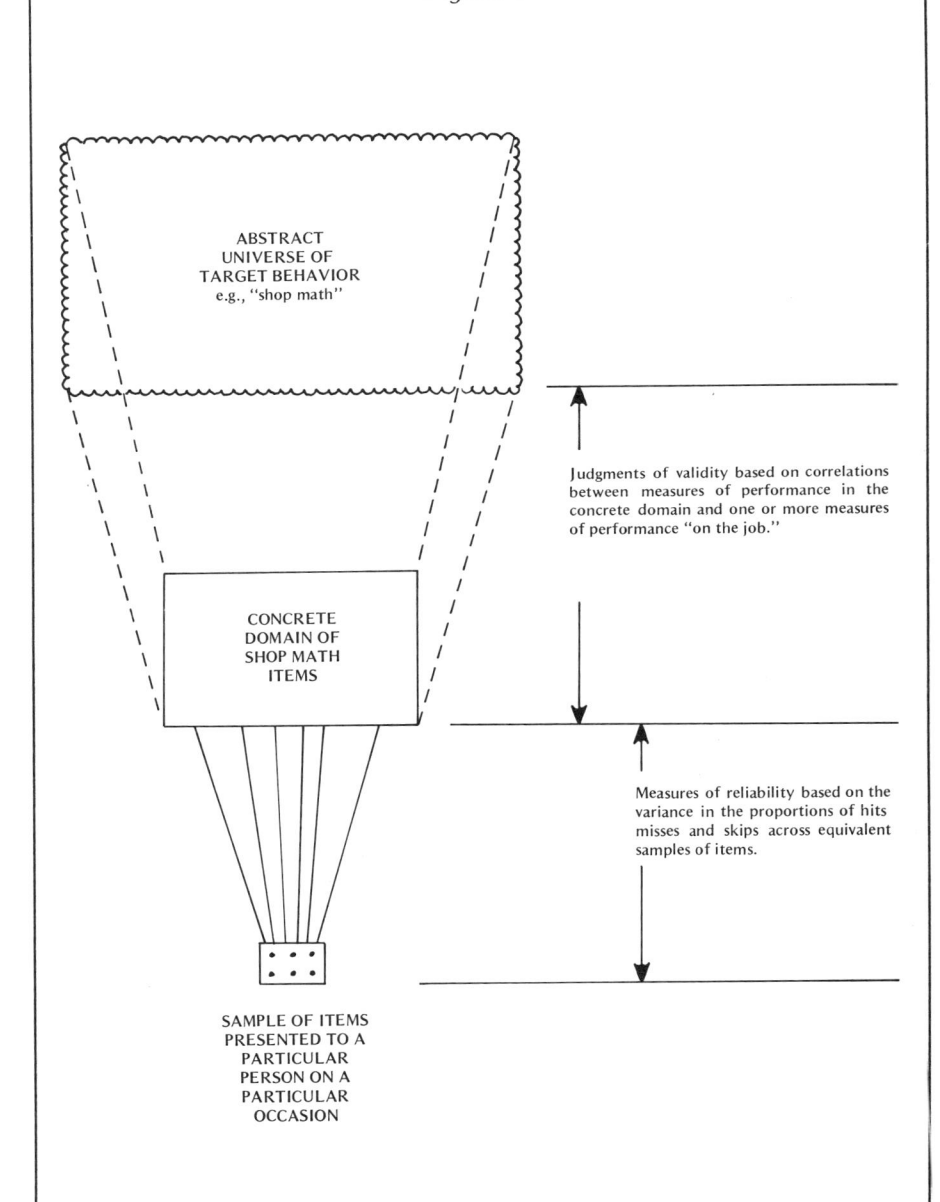

ABSTRACT
UNIVERSE OF
TARGET BEHAVIOR
e.g., "shop math"

Judgments of validity based on correlations between measures of performance in the concrete domain and one or more measures of performance "on the job."

CONCRETE
DOMAIN OF
SHOP MATH
ITEMS

Measures of reliability based on the variance in the proportions of hits misses and skips across equivalent samples of items.

SAMPLE OF ITEMS
PRESENTED TO A
PARTICULAR
PERSON ON A
PARTICULAR
OCCASION

the fact that in the DRT model a "domain" can never be defined in such a way as to include potential or nonexistent items. The potential or nonexistent items lie not in the domains but in the abstract universe of target behaviors. (In this emphasis, I disagree with Millman, Nitko and Johnson.)

It is also important to underline the fact that in DRT the inference that links the concrete domain with the abstract universe is one of transfer and generalization. Causation *is* implied in the correlations that link the hard- and soft-edged boxes. We wish to *generalize to* the abstract universe, not to predict in a normative or correlational sense. I believe that John Fremer is making a mistake in trying to lead us down the purely correlational path (Fremer, 1972).

**Frequent Misconceptions**

*False: Definition of domains has nothing to do with normative expectations.* We define domains of performance because we think somebody can accomplish them. Therefore, normative expectations must invariably enter into the initial choice of the abstract universe, or the selection of prototypical items. We *could* define a domain of performance nobody could accomplish, but it would be of little interest.

*False: Normative models cannot be superimposed on domains.* It is possible to draw samples from a concrete domain in such a way as to create norm-referenced scales of performance over the domain (if one wished to do so). Cronbach's generalizability theory (Cronbach, Rajaratnam and Gleser, 1963) provides the connecting link, and a study by Hively, Patterson and Page (1968) describes an application.

*False: Domain-referenced testing implies mastery learning.* The implication is the other way around. Mastery learning models imply the existence of domain-referenced testing procedures to determine mastery of each of the constituent domains in a learning hierarchy. However, it is not at all clear whether the most efficient way to acquire a repertoire (represented by a large domain) is to master each and every one of its constituents in a prescribed order (White, 1973).

*False: Domain-referenced testing is applicable to cognitive but not affective behavior.* Little research and development has yet been done in this area, but there are two clear lines of approach. The first is to conceptualize attitudes and interests as classes of behaviors that are evoked by general, non-directive stimulus conditions. We say someone "knows how" to read when he performs on call, but we say he is "interested in" reading when he reads spontaneously in a variety of situations. Thus, a domain for assessing interest in reading might involve an open-school setting in which students are encouraged to read in a variety of situations (on the school bus, in the lunchroom, and so forth) and where they are encouraged to read for a variety of purposes (as background for arts and crafts, field trips, etc.). The over-all frequency of words or pages read in these various broad (but well-defined) situations would then provide a measure of interest in reading.

A second approach to the "affective domain" is to study feelings of enthusiasm, boredom, anxiety, and so on, personally recorded by the learner in response to clearly specified stimulus conditions such as might be provided in film clips or role-play. This approach might be used, for example, in the development of domain-referenced tests of such things as attitudes toward drug use (Ahlgren, 1973; Duncan, Hively and Spence, 1974).

## Problems
### Setting Up
For the instructional technologist, the school administrator, teacher, learner or educational policy-maker, the technology of domain-referenced testing offers problems as well as opportunities. Foremost among the problems is that development of domain-referenced testing systems takes time, money and expertise. For the present, it is probably wise not to take big systems too seriously but to keep the basic model in mind and work with approximations. At present, those interested in practical applications would be wise to see a few, very general, domain-referenced measures of over-all growth in core areas like reading and mathematics, while encouraging teachers and students to create individually tailored miniature domains to objectify their immediate goals.

### Avoiding Conservativism
The potential conservative effect of large-scale domain-referenced testing is a serious problem. Since the development of a comprehensive domain-referenced testing system is time-consuming, it is likely to be focused on a very small part of the total school curriculum. If this likelihood is coupled with pressures for performance-based evaluation and accountability, the over-all effect may be to drive schools toward

very conservative programs. We need to work hard to find ways to encourage flexibility and individual initiative in generating domains and in tracking performance in them toward a variety of individual goals. The technology of domain-referenced testing can be used to help an institution define more precisely the behavior it expects of its members, or it can be used to help an individual define more precisely the goals toward which he alone is working. Ideally, it should do both.

*Communication*
Domain-referenced measures of performance are currently not easy to communicate. Even though the assumption may be spurious, many people seem to think they understand what is meant by "third-grade reading level" better than "ability to read aloud from a random sample of editorial pages at a hundred words per minute without skipping and with fewer than five mispronunciations." In order to give the latter measures appeal, we will have to anchor them to the behavior of prototypical persons or groups. For instruction, we need well-defined domains; for interpretation and validation, we need normative anchors.

**Some Practical Advice**
*To Product Developers*
We ought to concentrate first on clearly defining the behavioral domains to be associated with the products. Next we should provide a clear, but small-scale, demonstration that the products produce some worthwhile and replicable performance in that domain, by some well-described group of learners, in some well-described experimental situation. That should be enough: despite recent Office of Education policy, large-scale field trials designed to show the effects of the product across a wide population of users are not worthwhile. Users are bound to adapt products to an enormous variety of situations and learners. How they adapt them (given that they have been shown to work effectively somewhere for somebody) should be *their* problem. With a clear domain, some consultation from the developer and some experimental common sense, users can evaluate products much more efficiently than developers.

*To School Systems*
The immediate goal should be to encourage staff and students to

develop a variety of homemade, mutually agreed upon, domain-referenced measures of competence for each student's individual goals, and to work out ways to aggregate these to show the over-all productivity of the school system. In certain areas, such as reading and mathematics very general domain-referenced measures might be utilized, and computer based support systems like CAM may be helpful, but I would not wait for the installation of large master-learning systems.

*To Learners and Teachers*
For learners the problem is clear: unless you define your own domains of competence and prepare yourself for evaluation, you are bound to get pigeonholed by somebody else in ways that may not be comfortable. For teachers, as Popham implies, the problem is similar. If you do not get together with your students on the definition of such domains, and on measures of progress toward their mastery, you are likely to get evaluated on external criteria that you do not accept.

*To Citizens*
If you put pressure for educational accountability on school systems, teachers and students through the use of norm-referenced standardized tests, I believe you will get narrowly competitive and homogeneous education. Citizens can work productively with teachers and students to agree on basic domains of competence and to help insure that they can be acquired efficiently and happily. In the long run, of course, we are accountable, too.

## References

Ahlgren, A. Tests of Attitudes Toward Drug Use. Minneapolis, Minn.: Center for Educational Development, University of Minnesota, 1973.
Boulding, K. *The Image*. Ann Arbor, Mich.: University of Michigan Press, 1961.
Cronbach, L., N. Rajaratnam and G. Gleser. Theory of Generalizability: A Liberalization of Reliability Theory. *British Journal of Statistical Psychology*, 1963, *16*, 137-163.
Duncan, A.D., W. Hively and J. Spence. *Precise Personal Management and Precision Teaching: A Handbook for Humane Behaviorists*. New York: David McKay, 1974.
Fremer, J. Criterion-referenced Intepretations of Survey Achievement Tests. Educational Testing Service, Test Development memorandum, Princeton, N.J., 1972.
Glaser, R. A Criterion-Referenced Test. In Popham, W.J. (Ed.) *Criterion-Referenced*

*Measurement.* Englewood Cliffs, N.J.: Educational Technology Publications, 1971.

Hively, W., M.G. Maxwell, G.J. Rabehl, D.B. Sension and S. Lundin. *Domain-Referenced Curriculum Evaluation.* Los Angeles, Calif.: Center for the Study of Evaluation, University of California, 1973.

Hively, W., H. Patterson and S. Page. A Universe Defined System of Arithmetic Achievement Tests. *Journal of Educational Measurement,* 1968, *5*, 275-290.

Kuhn, T. *The Structure of Scientific Revolutions.* Chicago: University of Chicago Press, 1962.

Mager, R. *Preparing Instructional Objectives.* Palo Alto, Calif.: Fearon Publishers, 1962.

White, R. Research into Learning Hierarchies. *Review of Educational Research,* Summer 1973, *43*, 3.

# Some Helpful Sources

## Wells Hively

For the reader who may wish to gain a perspective on the field of domain-referenced testing, we offer the following bibliography (excluding many of the references previously cited in this issue). The citations in each section are arranged in historical, rather than alphabetical, order.

1. *Nothing is new under the sun:*

*Standards and Tests for the Measurement of the Efficiency of Schools and School Systems.* 15th Yearbook of the National Society for the Study of Education. Chicago: University of Chicago Press, 1916.

*The Measurement of Educational Products.* 17th Yearbook of the National Society for the Study of Education. Bloomington, Illinois: Public School Publishing Co., 1918.

2. *The classics of behavioral objectives:*

Tyler, R.W. *Constructing Achievement Tests.* Columbus, Ohio: Bureau of Educational Research, 1934.

Tyler, R.W. *Basic Principles of Curriculum and Instruction.* Chicago: University of Chicago Press, 1950.

3. *The uneasy alliance between behavioral objectives and norm-referenced testing:*

Lindquist, E.F. (Ed.) *Educational Measurement.* Washington, D.C.: American Council on Education, 1951. (The contrast between Lindquist's chapter and Thorndike's chapter in this volume vividly illustrates the struggle between the intuitive notion of DRT [Lindquist] and the intuitive notion of NRT [Thorndike]; a schizophrenia we have lived with ever since.)

4. *Roots of DRT in radical behaviorism*:

Skinner, B.F. *Verbal Behavior.* New York: Appleton-Century-Crofts 1957.

Skinner, B.F. Why We Need Teaching Machines. *Harvard Educational Review*, 1961, *31*, 377-398.

Markle, S.M. and P.W. Tiemann. *Really Understanding Concepts* Champaign, Illinois: Stipes Publishing Co., 1970.

5. *Behavioral objectives revisited*:

Tyler, R.W. et al. *Perspectives of Curriculum Evaluation.* AERA Monograph Series No. 1. Chicago: Rand McNally, 1967. (The articles by Gagné and Stake are of particular interest.)

Tyler, R.W. (Ed.) *Educational Evaluation: New Roles: New Means.* 68th Yearbook of the National Society for the Study of Education. Chicago: University of Chicago Press, 1969. (See especially the articles by Bloom and by Merwin and Womer.)

6. *The DRT-NRT controversy clarified*:

Bormuth, J.R. *On the Theory of Achievement Test Items.* Chicago: University of Chicago Press, 1970.

Popham, W.J. (Ed.) *Criterion-Referenced Measurement.* Englewood Cliffs, New Jersey: Educational Technology Publications, 1971.

Anderson, R.C. How to Construct Achievement Tests to Assess Comprehension. *Review of Educational Research*, 1972, *42*, 2, 145-170.

7. *The uneasy alliance, resolving, but still unresolved*:

Thorndike, R.L. (Ed.) *Educational Measurement* (Second Edition). Washington, D.C.: American Council on Education, 1971. (Contrast the articles by Cronbach and by Glaser and Nitko.)

JUL 13 1994

AUG 03 1994

SEP 6 1994

739